To   mum

Happy   Mother's

Hope enjoy

Tempus ORAL HISTORY *Series*

voices of
St Helens

Lots of love.

Gary. Pat,
Thomas & Hannah
x x x x

Ann, Joan and Mary – just three from a family of nine.

Tempus ORAL HISTORY *Series*

voices of
St Helens

Compiled by
David Paul

TEMPUS

First published 2000
Copyright © David Paul, 2000

Tempus Publishing Limited
The Mill, Brimscombe Port,
Stroud, Gloucestershire, GL5 2QG

ISBN 0 7524 2066 6

Typesetting and origination by
Tempus Publishing Limited
Printed in Great Britain by
Midway Clark Printing, Wiltshire

Children playing in the nursery at Lowe House School, 1954.

Contents

On site at Bold power station.

Acknowledgements

I would like to thank all the people of St Helens who have helped me to write this book, without whom it would not have been possible: Douglas Ashton, Henry Atherton, Agnes Bacon, Bill Barrow, Brenda Barrow, Josie Beard, Edith Blackmore, Iris Briscoe, Roy Burrows, Brian Coxhead, Jean Dale, Ken Dale, Beat Dingsdale, Tommy Dingsdale, Derek Gittins, Joan Gleave, Tom Gornall, Mary Green, Doris Hundley, Hannah Kelly, Mary Knox, John Lee, Harry Lynch, Roz Moore, Jack Rimmer, Bessie Roughley, Margaret Sill, Agnes Stirrup, Don Thornley, Margaret Winstanley, Vincent Woodward. I would also like to thank Stella Powell and Anne Marsh at Windle-Pilkington House and Eileen Lawrenson and Dot Rogers at Ruskin Lodge. Also, I am indebted to the people who loaned their treasured photographs and other mementoes, and in particular Chris Coffey and members of the Sutton Historic Society.

Finally, whilst I have tried to ensure that the stories are factually correct, not easy at the best of times, any errors or inaccuracies are mine alone.

One of the local pony club meetings.

Introduction

Without exceptions, this book has been written directly from the recorded memories of the people of St Helens. Tape recordings were made over a period of twelve months, with the generous participation of a huge range of townsfolk. It has to be said that some people were nervous to begin with, but, having sparked their imagination and re-kindled some of their memories, it was often difficult to get them to stop! It is clear that St Helens means a lot to a lot of people, and I hope that this is reflected in the book. Some people talked about the colliers of St Helens, or walking to Carr Mill Dam, whilst others spoke of working at Pilkington's, living through the Second World War, or getting the cane at school for the most trifling of misdemeanours. Whatever the memory, the generosity of spirit of the people was a common thread throughout. Time and again, reference was made to living through hard times with very little or no money – pushing a pram to the railway line to pick up coal that had dropped from the engines, or going to the market late on a Saturday evening to get a cheap

Father Gleave and mother Gleave with Ethel Smith and Milly Smith (children from mother Gleave's first marriage) and their own children Harold and baby Albert, 1923.

rabbit to make a stew – but there always seemed to be enough for the family across the road or the ageing aunt who lived on her own.

Since then there have been many social and economic changes, and today St Helens is a bustling town and a centre for retail, commercial and industrial activity. The town also acts as a focus for social events and draws people from many of the outlying villages and hamlets. My own abiding memory of when I first worked in St Helens more than thirty years ago, is how very welcoming the people were – and in that respect, nothing seems to have changed!

David Paul
St Helens, May 2000

CHAPTER 1

This is St Helens

Beechams clock tower – still one of the landmarks of St Helens.

Trams and Trolleybuses

At Hard Lane, where Skippers is now, is where the old trams and trolleybuses used to turn round. Every other one used to go through to Moss Bank and turn round there. The way they did that was they had this big bamboo cane, and they used to hook it on the line, pull it down, and then fix it to the next line, and the trolleybuses were then able to go back into town.

Ken Dale

Knives and Forks Chained Down

Every Sunday without fail, the place everybody used to go to was Carr Mill.

Proud parents in St Helens at the turn of the last century.

Everybody used to go in their Sunday best, and, being kids, you'd take a bottle of water and some jam butties. People just walked around, but it was the meeting place. It wasn't the thing for youngsters to go into pubs like they do now. I never went in a pub until I was twenty-one. They used to have a fair that came to Burkhill's Café which was just across the way from Carr Mill. It was a transport café – knives and forks used to be chained onto the benches so that nobody could pinch them, but nobody ever wanted to anyway! They were great big heavy things – you could hardly lift them up. There used to be a little fair visited every so often, so we used to go on that, but that was all of the entertainment that we got. As we got older

we used to go to so many dances. Also, Carr Mill had a club called The Cat's Whiskers. We used to go there every Friday, and they had all the groups – all the up and coming groups from Liverpool. It was just a lovely time to be young then. You never bothered about going out. I've walked from town across the fields opposite the Carr Mill Hotel – it's all housing now – at three o'clock in the morning without any fear at all.

Roz Moore

People of Eccleston

It's quite interesting, you find people now talking about living in old Eccleston. I was quite surprised when someone said that to me the other day, having discovered that old Eccleston was what I thought was council houses – superior council houses I might add, they were good, and a lot of very good people lived there.

Brian Coxhead

Paddy's Dole

I'm going to go back now to when my grandfather was alive, he lived down in Parr. Paddy Greenhough as they used to call him left some money, and all of the old people who had lived in Parr all of their life got, what my grandad called, Paddy Greenhough's dole. Each year, the ladies got a length of red flannel, and the men got half a crown for tobacco. I don't know whether it's still going or not, but with the interest that was on that money, it went on for years. To qualify, you had to have lived in Parr for all of your life. Now Paddy's Blunder was a different thing. Paddy's Blunder was Kurtz's Chemical Works – there's a ward in St Helen's hospital named after them. The chemical works blew up, and that's why it was called Paddy's Blunder. All the waste that came from there used to go like green jelly. My mother had a sister who got buried in it up to her waist. They came and asked my grandfather to come, as his daughter was buried in this liquor. Shortly afterwards she died of consumptive bowels, and they thought that it was because she was buried up to her waist. We all wore clogs in those days, and her clogs was still in there when they dragged her out. When I was a little girl, you used to be able to see the remains of Paddy's Blunder.

Edith Blackmore

Scarlet Fever

When I was about ten I had scarlet fever. I went into Peasley Cross Hospital and it was over the Christmas period. They took you away for a month then, and you couldn't see anybody. You could see your mum through a glass – I saw my mum just once. While I was in, it was awful. They used to come around with a tray and then comb your hair. They used to comb your hair with the nit combs and they had a little round tray and some cotton wool. They'd comb your hair and then take it off with cotton wool. I'd never known what it was like to have creepy-crawlies. I was full – they gave us a bath before we came home. I told my mother that I was in the bath and there were things crawling all over. There was a big to-do then

Nos 4 – 14 Edgeworth Street. Most gas lamps in this area were made at the Burrows Iron Foundry on Station Road, Sutton.

Sunday School Walking Day processing down Nutgrove Road in 1958 – trolleybuses were still running in St Helens at that time.

with the health. After I came out my mother whipped me back to the doctors. We were covered in lice and head lice. I was a bit poorly for a couple of days, but I did enjoy my stay there. Around Christmas, all of the others who were getting better could sit at a long table for their meal, but I'd been pretty sick, so I had to stay in bed. I was given a cloth rabbit as a present – that was my Christmas present in 1943.

Jean Dale

Into the 'Dolly Blue'

We lived at the bottom of Oxford Street and there was eight of us and we all went to York Street School, then we went to St Mary's Church of England School. We never had anything, so one of my sisters always used to go in the middens to see what she could find. She didn't need to do, but she did. It was always first up, best dressed. We all left school at fourteen. Some worked at UGB, I worked at Fosters and then I went to Triplex. At the bottom of Oxford Street there was a laundry, and some girls worked in here for very little money. There was also the picture house in Oxford Street that they also used to hang around. There used to be a little church there, the Oxford Hall, where we all went – our mother used to send us out of the way. We used to sing hymns and what have you. Eventually, because we were overcrowded, they moved a few out. But, ours was a three-bedroomed house, we were lucky. We had some sleeping in the parlour, but that's all we could do because of the overcrowding. People came around checking on who was overcrowded in those days. The people themselves always seemed to be a lot better than what they are today. You were never stuck for anything. If you hadn't got anything, even though they didn't have anything, but we'd all help one another. I've gone to gasworks with a pram to collect coke. I've pulled it along Duke Street. We also had a boiler in the yard, it was for the washing. We used to have two tubs and a bath with 'dolly blue' in. We used to have to 'dolly' them, put them through the mangle and then shove them into the boiler, and then when they came out they went in the 'dolly blue'. It used to take us at least two days to do the washing and ironing. When we used to come home from school, mum would tell us to go into the wash house, and we used to have to turn the mangle.

Brenda Barrow

The 'Sunshine Houses'

I was born and bred in St Helens. I lived, right up to being married, at Thatto Heath in Elephant Lane. I lived right opposite what is now Tannery Farm Garage, in what they called the 'Sunshine Houses', which were built very much in a hurry I think, round about 1939 at the beginning of the

Step houses in Robins Lane. In the foreground can be seen the 'middle steps' which led up to Mucky Alley. They were also a shortcut to Worsley Brow.

13

Three generations of the Critchley family in the backyard of No. 14 Peel Street.

war. They were generally one of the very many 'jerry-built' properties around in those days. Where Tannery Farm Garage is now was actually a farm at the time, and we used to get our milk from there, and the milkman had a handcart – not even a horse. He used to push the handcart around. You wouldn't getaway with it these days because of all of the legislation on lifting and handling, but that's what they did in those days. Elephant Lane was a fairly quiet area, it wasn't until I was about five that we started getting buses coming up. It was a big new thing then going on a bus. Prior to that, if you wanted to get a bus into St Helens, you had to walk down to

Nutgrove Road, Thatto Heath Road – that area. Although having said that, in the better weather in the summer, my mother would always walk across the fields – right down past the old brick works and the tea-pot works that were there, and going into St Helens that way. But, unlike today, you had all of the shops locally. I can remember shopping for my mother when I was six or seven years old on a Saturday morning, going to the grocers. From there we got the veg. and all of the rest of the bits. Along the lane they had just about everything, so the only time that we went into town, especially, was to get clothes from Marks & Spencer's and Christmas shopping for toys in Woolworth's. It really had to be a special event to go up to town. And, to go to anywhere further afield to places like Liverpool – well, that was abroad! It was almost unheard of. I can't remember in my childhood anyone in our family going to Liverpool for shopping. The only time that I went to Liverpool is when we went to see my aunt who lived in Llandudno. It was myself, my younger sister and two other cousins who used to go on a day trip – sailing on the St Tudno. That was about the only time that I ever went into Liverpool as a kid. It was a big day out, and something to look forward to.

Vincent Woodward

A Girl off Brown's Bread Van

My husband worked for forty-six years at Pilks, he retired when he was sixty. When I met him I was working on the bread van for Browns. I met him at his garden gate. He used to take the bread off me, and then one Sunday night – after we'd been parading down Prescot Road when I was about eighteen – I met his cousin. Well, my husband used to go to the Parish Church Men's Class on a Sunday afternoon, and his cousin did. They must have been discussing where they'd been the night before. He said that he'd met a girl off Brown's bread van. Norman said that he knew who he meant, as she came to their house. He asked me for a date, but the first night I couldn't tell him, because we had a man driving, and I was scared stiff of him. Anyway, eventually, we courted for four years. He came from Windle Hurst. We had our sixtieth wedding anniversary, and we had a telegram from the Queen, and we had a family gathering in the centre where I live – I live in sheltered accommodation. We were living in our own house in Nutgrove in Govett Road, and I have one daughter who is a schoolteacher. I never said anything to her, but I applied for the flat. Pilkingtons built them at Haresfinch. We went in there – I was eighty then and my husband was eighty-two. We had a good happy married life, but my husband ended up with Alzheimer's, and I had to let him go into Victoria Nursing home at Rainford. He was in there for eight months, and then he died. He was a good husband, and we had a good loving relationship.

Hannah Kelly

A Pennyworth of Fish

I started work when I was fourteen, earning eight [shillings] and a penny a week. You took your money home and then you just gave it to your mother. She then gave you back your 'spends'. My mother gave me a shilling in bright new pennies. I kept them in my pocket for ages. Mind you, you could get a dozen eggs for threepence. We could go to the theatre or the Hippodrome, we used to go in the gods – that was threepence. Then we went to the chip shop just across the road from the pictures, and we'd have a pennyworth of fish and a twopenny fish. They were always wrapped in newspapers. Then you'd get on the bus, a penny for the bus, and you'd still have money left out of the shilling – and you'd had a good night out.

Douglas Ashton

I Was the Little Skivvy

I used to go to Knowsley Road School which is knocked down now. Sometimes I think that I must have had a better childhood than some of the others. If anyone wanted anything doing, like child-minding, then my mum used to always say that I would do it. I used to do all kinds of things like scrubbing steps. I used to be the little skivvy. We used to play with the lads. I have a stepbrother and a stepsister. We had a two-bedroomed house. My sister and I had a bed between us, and my brother had a little bed on his own. The walls were all done in distemper, green distemper upstairs. It was lovely being able to write on the walls with your finger – my mother used to go mad. We used to have a bed with knobs on all of the corners, and we used to get the bedcovers, and we'd fasten it on as either a tent or a bath. We were poor and I wasn't allowed to go in for the scholarship, but my sister passed for Cowley.

Bessie Roughley

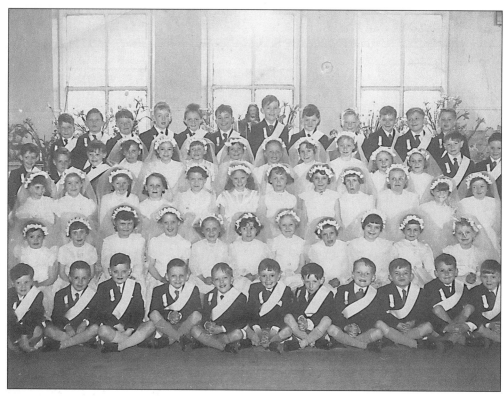

Happy boys and girls after making their first communion.

We Didn't Know About VD

They were good days for us, but they must have been terrible days for our parents. When you see what the position now of these young married couples, they complain about the housework and this, that and the other, they don't know how lucky they are! Wash days in those days used to be a full day. You'd come home from school and there'd be washing on the line – the whole place stunk of washing. When we were kids we didn't need pocketfuls of money to enjoy ourselves like the kids do these days. We enjoyed ourselves with simple things. When we used to be on holiday from school, a month in summer, we used to go camping in sack tents. It was so enjoyable. We were,

compared with these days, we were so innocent – we didn't know what a homosexual was, we'd never heard the term. We were stupid as regards sex. We didn't know about VD or anything like that, it was only when I was in the army that they used to show us slides.

Henry Atherton

Married at Nineteen

I was married at nineteen. My husband was in the army. We had to get married, I might as well tell you that, because I was always a rum un. I had four kiddies and I've reared three. I've got a good few grandchildren and great grandchildren. With kids these days they want money all of the time. They get no pleasure now unless they've got a fistful of money. We had to go and make our own fun. We'd run with a ball – and a paper ball rolled up with string, kicking it from one end of the street to the other. Sometimes we'd throw a rope over the lamp and start swinging on that until the neighbours shifted us.

Josie Beard

Lots of Picture Houses

We had lots of picture houses in those days, but there's none now. it was a question of which one shall we go to – the Scala; the Oxford; the Palladium; the Hippodrome; the Rivoli; the Savoy; the Capital – but now there's nothing.

Ken Dale

Money Was Scarce

My happiest time was when I got married in St Luke's at Knowsley Road. We didn't go away because money was scarce then. I just went to my sister's house because she wasn't living there. We just went for the weekend and later on we went to Wales. I met my husband at Kirkland Street Dance Hall – we used to go there on a Saturday night. My

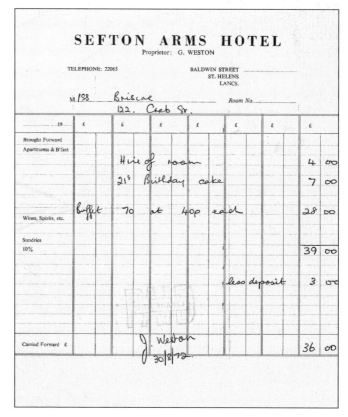

The cost of a good twenty first 'Do' in 1972!

A procession walking from Peckershill Road end of Robins Lane, c. 1985.

husband came from Sutton Manner and I was twenty-one when I got married. We went to live with my mother when I first got married.

Doris Hundley

Made the First Glass Brick

I was born in St Helens, I was born in Eldon Street. I went to a great school, St Thomas's School. I was christened there, confirmed there and married there. I got married when I was twenty and I lived in Borough Road, and I still live there, in the same house. I've been there sixty-three years in June. My husband worked at Ravenhead, and he also made the first glass brick that they ever made. I've had a nice time really. We lived facing the Kimick

and the sand beds. Everyone used to call it the Kimick, and of course there were the sand beds. There's houses on there now facing me. I had three children – two boys and a girl. Two of them went to Cowley, and one boy went to higher grade.

Margaret Winstanley

Our Bathroom Was a Luxury

When I was fourteen we moved up to Portico and then of course we had a bath in the house. Our bathroom was a luxury in those days. That was in 1937. Tommy lived further down, they lived at No. 7 and we lived at No. 29. The house isn't there now – they found an underground spring. That was after we'd left. They were built in rows of four, the two end houses had three bedrooms, and the two in the middle were four bedrooms, because there was an entry down the middle, and that meant that there could be an extra room in both houses. They were downstairs bathrooms of course, not upstairs.

Beat Dingsdale

Trolleybuses Were Quiet

I went to Robins Lane School in Sutton that's near the Sutton Park. When I was growing up it was all open fields by Sutton Park. All this place wasn't there then, and the centre of St Helens wasn't like it is now. Where you have the Church Square now, where St Helen's Church is, just by Woolworth's and Marks and Spencer's – it's a pedestrian way now. When I was at school, there was buses running along there, and at the top end there was a shop called Hart's, and that was all bric-a-brac, you used to be able to get anything there – cheap!

The trolleybuses were running then, I haven't seen a trolleybus running in St Helens for donkey's years. Going back to the war and just before, the trolleybuses were running in St Helens. They used to go to Parr, Sutton, Haydock and other places. When I was at school, if we went to visit relatives in Parr, we used to catch a bus in Sutton. First we used to walk into Sutton, and then we used to catch a trolleybus into Parr. They were much better than buses today, they were electric. If you got on a trolleybus there wasn't a sound. When you got on a tram in Manchester or Liverpool – until recently they had trams in Liverpool – all you could hear was clank, clank, clank. It was just like being on a train. With a trolleybus, having tyres, there was no sound – no sound at all. You could sit on the bus, and if you weren't talking you just sat quiet, and you wouldn't hear a sound. You could hear the birds singing in the trees as we went past, because there was no sound at all.

Don Thornley

Agnes Bacon and her husband. She was 8th St Helens Girl Guides captain from 1941 until 1948.

19

It was at this house, No. 14 Grimshaw Street, that John Coffey won the first ever Treble Chance on Littlewoods Pools. He won £75,000 for scoring twenty three points in 1950.

Waiting for the wedding – St Mark's church, 1962.

Safe at Night

Well what I think was good about life was, you could leave doors open years ago. You didn't hear about any rape or women getting beaten up. You could leave doors open and nothing happened. I also liked the cobbled streets. Today you have to rise with the times, but I don't think that everything's as good as in the past. Years ago it was far better than it is now. I think it was because I used to be able to walk – when my kiddies were little, about forty-odd years ago, I used to be able to walk through Vicky Park at eleven o'clock at night coming home with the two kiddies in the pram, and you felt safe and knew nothing would happen to

you. I had a sister-in-law that lived up at Hard Lane way, and I used to walk through Vicky Park, and nothing ever happened to you. And, there was more entertainment for the younger ones than there is now. There was pictures, cinemas all over the place, and there were lots of different dance halls. There's none now. I think that life was better then than it is now.

Iris Briscoe

Clean Steps and Windows

People used to clean their steps with the donkey-stone. They used to go out every day and donkey-stone the step. Everybody's fronts were swilled every day and the ledges wiped, and you used to see ladies sat out on the sash windows upstairs cleaning the windows. I always thought that they were going to fall out. Nobody ever paid for window cleaners.

Roz Moore

Pilkington's Houses

I don't remember much about my parents, only that my mum and dad lived in Folds Lane at the bottom of Leach Lane, and they used to live in what they called Pilkington's houses. Before that my mum lived in 14 Peel Street at the beginning at the top of College Street. They were pulled down and they built new houses there, so she moved into a flat a Folds Lane, and they were Pilk's when they were first built – Margaret Pilkington

had a lot to do with them. Later they were sold to the council. I used to work twelve-hour shifts, three days on and three days off. I also did overtime, but I always used to go to my mum and dad's. Many's the time that I've finished work at seven and gone straight down to my mum's. My dad had a colostomy bag, but he died, so I went along to my mum's a couple of times a week. She died in 1980.

Iris Briscoe

Didn't Want Me to Work

I had to go and find a job when I was fourteen. It was difficult finding a job. I used to go trudging around all over the place. Sometimes I used to go home and say that I'd been to places and said that they didn't want anybody. I ended up in a fruit, veg. and fish shop until I was twenty-one – I got

Victoria Square as it used to be.

No. 594 St. Helens, May 12 1911			
M Wm Booth			
Please receive of GRIFFINS, LIMITED, ARTISTS AND PHOTOGRAPHERS, Ormskirk Street and Westfield Street.			
2 Rockers 3/6 4 Chairs 20/-	2	7	6
Table 22/6 Sofa 43/	3	4	6
Rug 10/6 Fender 13/6	1	4	-
Tidy 7/6 2 Tidy 4/-	-	13	6
2 C Chairs	-	9	6
2 Pans 5/2 Kettle 4/6	-	9	8
7½ yds Oilcloth	1	2	6
Top Bar	-	6	-
	9.	17	2

Just £9 17s 2d to furnish a complete house in 1911.

married then. My husband didn't want me to go out working, so I didn't. He went in the forces two years after we got married. I had a son then, so there was no way that I could go out working. I regret now that I never had to go out to work. Sometimes I think that I was lucky.

Bessie Roughley

Critchley's Televisions

I went to St Austin's School. Initially, the infants was in Crown Street – it's no longer there – right by Thatto Heath Labour Club. Funnily enough that's still there, but then drinking places stay forever don't they! As I've mentioned before, there were shops with everything that we needed in Elephant Lane, in one way or another. There was the fish merchant, three chip shops, two newsagents, a couple of butchers, a bakery, a pet shop, and even an electrical shop – so, when this new wonder-thing came in called television, we used to go and stand by the window and watch these televisions. That was Critchley's down the bottom of Elephant Lane on the corner of South Street.

Vincent Woodward

We All Had to Be Clogged

At night we always used to have gruel. We had a big iron pan – there was no stove or anything like that – and that would be on the fire. Anybody who came in would get a cup of tea and a huge bowl of gruel. Sometimes we'd have hotpot, oxtail or rabbit. There were always hearts and things like that cooking away. We were never actually short of food, but it was all cheap stuff. My dad worked at UGB, and we had six girls and two boys, but he could never have a drink, because he couldn't afford it – he had to clog all of us. He used to come in from UGB, have a wash and then go to bed. That was all that he did. The first time that I can remember my dad going into a pub was when one of my sisters got married. We just didn't have the money, not like people have it today.

Brenda Barrow

So Many Fruit Pastilles

When I was fourteen I met a young man who'd come to work at the Maypole, the grocers. I was also helping Arthur Hodges and his wife who'd opened a wholesale sweets and tobacco. This faced the Maypole, in the main street in Earlestown, and I said that if I had any spare time then I would come and help them. I liked this kind of work, and I was good at it. So I used to give her a few hours as well. There was no closing at half five like it is now. Occasionally – no, more than occasionally, this young man that worked in the Maypole used to come over for fruit pastilles. I thought that he ate a lot of fruit pastilles, he was always coming in for a tube of fruit pastilles. I was always singing. I was in every choir that there was. I found out, eventually, that this boy also liked singing. He asked me to go to the pictures with him. I said that when it was my half-day, I would meet him in St Helens. I met him and he asked if we could go to the theatre instead, as it was Carol Levis's Discoveries. He took a piece of music out of his inside pocket – I didn't know that he

Ethel Marsh of Mill Lane and John Sharples of Robins Lane on the banks of Mill Dam, 1920s.

A social gathering of the darts league at the Wheatsheaf.

could sing. I wouldn't go, so we went to the pictures instead. I could have killed myself after, when I knew how well he could sing. He was a beautiful singer. After we were married I asked him how he felt when I stopped him, but he said that it didn't matter too much.

Joan Gleave

Bombs Over St Helens

A bomb dropped at the top of our street, Morgan Street, where I lived. In Parr, two men were killed, a Mr Burke and a Mr Green – his daughter still lives near me at Sutton. All of our windows were out. I went to my uncles, because he had one of those table shelters. My dad took us down there, and we could hear the chugging of the German aeroplanes. The mobile guns were after him, and he got rid of his bombs over St Helens – in Somerset Street and then in Morgan Street. Mr Green had a little dog named Nigger, and it ran when the bomb dropped where his master got killed, and when the next bomb dropped in Fleet Lane, which was quite a distance away, the dog got killed there.

Edith Blackmore

Half-a-Crown For a Win

My grandad played for the 'Saints'. They used to play at Littler's Field before they played at Knowsley Road. They got half a crown when they won, but nothing when they got beat!

Margaret Winstanley

A Bathroom with a Toilet Upstairs

When I was about six we moved to one of the new houses that had been built in Clinkham Wood. There was a huge garden which we'd never had before, and there was a bathroom with a toilet upstairs and one downstairs. I couldn't wait to get into this bath – so my dad filled this bath. First he'd had to light the fire to heat the water which took a couple of hours, so he did this because I wanted the bath. As soon as he filled it I was frightened to get in! It was a huge thing, and I was used to being in the sink. So he let the water out and took me downstairs to get into the sink, but I wouldn't get into that either because I wanted a bath! Well, this went on for an hour. In the finish I got my legs rapped and I didn't get a wash at all. I was so fascinated with this bath, it was wonderful – but, at the same time, I was a bit frightened of this huge white thing. I'd always been used to standing up with somebody holding on to me. The first time that I did get a bath, I hung onto the sides – clinging on for dear life! It seems strange now because I love my bath. It wasn't just a bathroom and a toilet in our new house, we had a separate kitchen and dining room and sitting room – and, I had a bedroom all to myself. That was in 1948. My uncle, who had a coal business, moved us in his lorry – and the coal was still in the back!

Roz Moore

Envelope Secretary

I was in Nutgrove Methodist church. I started off as a youth leader, then I was in the Sunday School as a teacher, I was a JMA secretary – that's missionary work, then, after that I was a steward, a communion steward, and then I was the envelope secretary. I've had a very active life.

Hannah Kelly

A Pan of Pea Soup

Years ago when we lived in Peel Street, all we could see was other people that lived by us. They used to have short curtains, and they used to lift up the corner and peep out. Nothing ever happened without one of your neighbours finding out what you were doing. You couldn't do anything secret because they were all watching you, but I do remember, if your mum was ever ill or not well and she had to go to bed, you could knock at any door, or they'd shout over and give you a jam butty, or they'd send a pan of soup over for you to have. People were very clannish years ago. I know that they reckon it was the bad old days, and these are the good days, but I think that those times were better. No children needed to go hungry, because there'd always be some neighbours that would send you over some pea soup or something. Anyway, shops used to sell pans of pea soup years ago. You used to be able to go in shops and you could take a dish and they'd fill it with pea soup or anything, but they don't do it now.

Iris Briscoe

Mrs Greers' Nettle Pop

In Elephant Lane where we lived, there was a woman called Mrs Greers, and she used to

The 'first born' – 1950.

make nettle pop, and it was only a penny a bottle.

Tommy Dingsdale

Up in the Gods

Every single night of the week you could go and see a different picture. There used to be the Hippodrome in Corporation Street and the Rivoli. Then there was the Savoy and the Capital. Then there was what they called the Parr Dog – I don't know the real name of it. Then there was the Sutton Bug, and the man on the door was called Persil – and you daren't fall out with Persil otherwise he wouldn't let you in! And then we had the Oxford which is now the Plaza, the Scala which is now Lennons, the Empire in Thatto Heath, the Palladium in Boundary Road. You could go and see a different picture every single week. They had one in Billinge that was made from corrugated iron. We used to wait until the picture started, and then we used to run past with sticks – it made a real racket inside! They'd call the police now! Then there was the Theatre Royal, but all we could afford was the 'gods'. You were that far up, that even if you saw anything you certainly couldn't hear anything.

Roz Moore

We Lived On Fish

My dad's family had a fish shop on North Road, and everybody knew Aunty Gwenny. We'd see her every morning as she was going to the railway station for the fish. We lived on fish because we used to get it for nothing.

Roz Moore

The Clog and Stocking Fund

There used to be an organisation called The Clog and Stocking Fund, so-called because people used to give money in for charity, and it was for holidays for the children of

Sherdley Hall Farm – originally built as yeomen's cottages.

Catching up on the news after a visit to Morrisons!

poor families. I went on one of them to Betws-y-Coed in Wales. There was a waterfall, and at night when we were all in these huts which had been specially built, all you could hear was owls hooting – I wanted to go back home!

Tommy Dingsdale

Seven Brothers and One Sister

I had seven brothers and one sister. We all got on very well, but it was only a two-bedroomed house that we lived in. All the lads slept in one room, and my mam and my dad and my sister slept in the other. Times have changes a bit now. I don't think that things have gone any better – if anything, it's gone worse!

John Lee

Home for Seven O'clock

I had a very strict father. I always had to be in for seven o'clock at night – summer and winter. All of the others used to be playing out, but I had to come in at seven o'clock. And, when I was courting at sixteen, I still had to be in at nine o'clock. My father was a good man, but very strict with us – me and my brother. There was only my brother and me – I lost him in the war, my brother, at Dunkirk. But, we had a lovely time together.

Margaret Winstanley

I Fitted Gas Masks

At sixteen I became an air raid wardens messenger – that was in the early days of the war. The air raid warden was a man named Mr Cushioner, and he was a jeweller in the town centre. The main air raid warden was a man named Eric Physian, and he was a tobacconist. I fitted gas masks in the town, and then I was called up at eighteen and went to Queens Barracks at Perth for training. That was in the Black Watch. When I came back from there I joined the Seventh Armoured Division – the Dessert Rats, in Oxford. Then, off I went across on the 'big one'. At the end of the war I got married, and then after the war I did twelve months in Venice, Italy with the army.

Bill Barrow

Made Bread on a Monday

When we were little they used to have road cleaners, not like they have today, it was like a big lorry and there was a bar on the back with holes in it, and they used to drive up the road, and it used to go right across the road, and all water used to be coming out, and they'd be washing all the road, and the children used to be running around getting their feet sopping wet as they chased it. There was a similar one, but that used to spread tar all over the road. You couldn't go on it until it dried, but in summer it all came up in little bubbles, and we used to crack these little bubbles with our fingers and our feet, and we'd get told off when we got in. Then there was hoopla, where we trundled a hoop, and at other times we'd play top and whip – we broke one or two windows with that! Then we used to go on a field where there was a big rope, and we used to swing

The cost of a funeral in 1943.

Ladies always wore hats then!

on it and then throw ourselves off into the lake. I used to get into an awful lot of trouble with my parents, but our parents always seemed to be better. They used to look after you proper, with rags in your hair, and the sandals would be whitened all in a row for the morning. On Saturday afternoon, all of the baking stuff would come out, and the apple pies and the Eccles cakes would be made. She used to bake in the oven at the side of the fire, and if ever you were cold, it wasn't a hot water bottle, it was a shelf wrapped up in a towel or something. She used to make bread on a Monday. We had trips to New Brighton with tomato butties, and they were all soggy when we got there, but we used to love it.

Mary Knox

CHAPTER 2

Growing Up

Rachel Ashton of No. 27 Fisher Street. Her husband, Isaac was the local blacksmith, undertaker and cab driver.

Grandma Made Our Fronts

I was born at Thatto Heath which is a district of St Helens. My memories of that age are living in a terraced house, the toilets were right at the end of the yard, the lighting was gas – I think that it was called a gas mantle, it looked like a kind of banana. I used to go to my Grandma's a lot, Grandma Taylor, because mother was always working, like they

did in those days. One day it was doing the washing, next day it was doing the ironing, so I used to go up to my Grandma's, and in fact, a lot of people thought that my name was Tommy Taylor and not Tommy Dingsdale – I was there that often! I always remember that my Grandma had an oil lamp, they had oil there in those days, and she used to knit socks for my elder brother and me. You'd see a ring of wool, and then the sock would then start to grow, coming down underneath. Also, she used to make what we call a 'front'. It was like a jersey, but it was only a front piece with a collar on. So you had this collar, the front piece, and then when you put a pullover on, it looked as though you had a jersey on. Everybody was poor.

Tommy Dingsdale

There Were That Many Pubs

I was born in St Helens, and lived for most of my life about a mile away in Doulton Street, although I actually lived in Westfield Street at my grandmothers when I was born in 1935. The house I lived in Westfield Street is covered by the road out to Liverpool on the Liverpool-bound carriageway. My earliest memory – well, I can't remember very much about living there apart from this period during the war, and as some of the roads in St Helens then were – talk about find your way by the pubs, there were that many pubs, if you had half a pint in everyone, then you'd be drunk before you got to the end. My grandmother lived next to a pub, and what struck me during the war was that all of these houses had cellars, and it's quite interesting in that they had a trapdoor into the cellar if there was a bar next door – I might add that the cellar door was always locked, this was long before I got to the stage of enjoying a pint. That's my bit about Westfield Street, but round about there, I've just about got memories of this. I always had shoes and was looked after. I suppose that compared to someone like Tommy Dingsdale, I don't suppose that I ever had it rough, because one wasn't poor when compared to people that you saw around you. My parents were buying their

own house in Doulton Street which isn't far from here. It was a bit unusual in those days, because a lot of people lived in rented or council accommodation, so we felt a bit better off – we had a bathroom and an inside toilet which not everybody had, although most of those houses have been improved quite a bit since then.

Brian Coxhead

Dad's Cold Cure

I was born in St Helens, but we moved to Clinkham Wood, but the buses only went to the bottom of the hill, so you had to walk from there, but if it was snowing, you very often had to walk all the way into town. I daren't tell my dad that I had a cold, because he made you walk, insisting that it was good for a cold, the fresh air. So you kept it to yourself.

Roz Moore

North Wales For Holidays

We used to walk either down to Toll Bar or along to where McClean & Appleton used to be, and get the bus to Prescot, and then get the No. 10 from Tinling's the printers in Prescot to Liverpool. Tinling's used to do a lot of the magazine-type things like the *Radio Times* – there wasn't a *TV Times* in those days of course, it was just the *Radio Times*. A lot of the women's magazines were printed there. Going to Liverpool was a big day out, and then getting the ferry to Llandudno. The boat itself then used to go on along the Menai Straights, and I always had this dread of it never coming back, and we'd have to spend the rest of our lives in Llandudno. It's funny, but myself and my wife still go to Llandudno very regularly for short breaks or holidays. I've always liked it right from the word go. Obviously, I think that most people in this area probably associate the North Wales coast as the holiday place – certainly people of my age anyway.

Vincent Woodward

Street Games

When I was in Eldon Street we used to play all sorts. Like I say, my uncle worked at

Before the Walking day in 1959. Claire Gleave with her friend and younger brother Andrew.

the ropery, and he used to always bring me good ropes to play skipping with, and our mother, she used to turn up for us at night, so that we could skip. Of course, we played top and whip, and my brother did as well – he played top and whip. We also played what they called 'stonies'. I had a relative who used to bring me 'stonies' from UGB. We had all sorts really.

Margaret Winstanley

Digging for Victory

Thatto Heath Council School during the war, when it was 'Dig For Victory', gave us our own little plot, and I got more education there about growing things than I could have got from many of the colleges today. Everything was relevant then. They taught us all about the four-year cycle and things like that. In the war years that was it, everyone was encouraged to 'Dig For Victory'. When I went up to the secondary school it was the same there, and, even after the war they did it for a while. It's understandable with all of our ships being sunk – we needed to grow as much as we could. Most of the food we had was vegetables, there was very little 'fancy' food. We were also encouraged to keep pigs, so we had a plot where we kept pigs and hens. As I said, we had a Yorkshire range, but the ovens were never very efficient, so I used to use it for hatching the chickens. The only trouble was, when I hatched them all out, I didn't want to part with them! We used to have little chickens all around the house. When they were eventually taken off me I used to cry my eyes out.

Tom Gornall

A Sad Growing Up

There were eight of us and I was in the middle. My sister was the eldest and then my brother, and then there was another sister and then me. It was a sad growing up.

Doris Hundley

No Television or Radio

I came to St Helens when I was about two years old, and I've been here ever since. We lived at New Town, in Brontë Street. My father worked at Pilkington Brothers, he was a driver – it was horses then. We were brought up in a terraced house in Brontë Street. As children we played whip and top and various things like that. We played games that we made up ourselves. There was no such thing as going to the pictures or television or radio or anything like that. It was just our own games.

Jack Rimmer

Sunday School Every Sunday

I went to the Sacred Heart School, which was a Catholic school. We had no choice in those days – you had to go to Sunday School every Sunday afternoon. If you didn't then the priest would be walking up and down, and then you had to go in. School was OK. We had one teacher and she was a bugger! Maggie Frane we used to call her, Miss Frane. We were all rum uns in those days, we got away with murder.

Josie Beard

A young man dressed ready for his first communion, 1960.

Woken up by the Clogs

Going back to my own home life in Elephant Lane, it was on the main route going to all of the collieries, all the pits. I can remember that nearly every morning you'd be woken up by all the colliers with their clogs on walking down past our house. They used to walk down there towards Sutton Heath. My dad was a miner of course, and he worked at either the Queen Pit or the King Pit, I can't quite remember the name. The pits had different names then, but I always remember them walking down, but that's all gone now – it's ancient history.

Tommy Dingsdale

Jim Taylor and Minnie Moran at their wedding, outside St Anne's Presbytery.

They'd Find Her a Cell for the Night

When I was a girl, there were three children – a boy older than myself, then I came along, and then I had a little sister. During that time my mother's sister and her husband – he came from Staffordshire and worked on the canal bank for a Staffordshire firm – he brought with him TB and gave it to his wife. She opened a business at the bottom of Peter Street, near to Liverpool Road. They were doing very well when her husband died of TB and shortly after, so did she. The two children were left. My dad was working for a firm on the canal bank, and they offered him a job 'bossing' in Widnes, but it would mean that the family would have to move out there, and if they couldn't take the two little orphans with them, then my mother

wouldn't go. But they couldn't – for some reason they couldn't take them away so quickly. So, my dad didn't get the job. He wasn't really upset about it, he was a man that took everything that was coming, and he met one of his old bosses as he went home after he'd been told this. The boss said for him to come along the following day, and he'd have a job for him. He started work on the following day, and they took on the two children, a boy and a girl, and that made five of us. We were living in Central Street them. We three were born in Gleave Street, and then we went to live in Birchley Street, but mother didn't like all of the steps that led down from Birchley Street onto the main road, so they went into Central Street, but the house wasn't big enough, and we landed in Peter Street. The business was sold, that auntie had had, and we all went together, and that was it –

that was our home then. One day, mother was going out for a pint of milk, and she found a girl crying on the corner. She asked her what was the matter. The girl said she'd gone on her holidays to Scotland to another of her mother's sisters, and while she was away, the auntie that she was living with was upset. She didn't think that Mary was coming back. My mother told her to wait, while she went to see her husband and see what he thought. He told her to go to the police and they'd find her a cell for the night, but my mother knew that he was only teasing her, 'codding' as we used to call it. He said, as she was going out through the door, to tell the girl that she would have to sleep with the other children. Mother wondered whether they kept a lot of children in the cells! Mother came back with the girl, and that was the beginning of Mary's life with us. My mother's mother died and left a young daughter, so they took her as well. There were seven of us, and we all lived a very happy life. My mother was an ex-nurse. She was called on by all of the neighbours if there was anything wrong, because in those days, paying a doctor was something you did on a weekly basis – nobody had enough money to pay doctors out of their money. They had to save up for everything.

Margaret Sill

Shopkeepers Had Time to Chat

I used to like going shopping. We used to go a lot to the Co-Op in Cooper Street, and I liked having conversations with the people who were serving you – and they had the time to chat. They don't do now, you go through these checkouts, and they ring up the tills, and they don't have time to talk to you, which shopkeepers did years ago. It was a lot better as well.

Iris Briscoe

The Slipper Baths

I lived in Albion Street, in fact I was born in Albion Street. I had four brothers and it was a terraced house that we lived in, with no baths. My dad used to light the boiler in the wash house to heat the water so that it could be tipped into the tin bath. We had a wash house – a lot of houses didn't – but we had a wash house. It was an old-fashioned copper and the fire was made underneath. We filled it up with coal so that we could boil the clothes, but it was also used for other things as well, one being baths. We lived around the corner from Boundary Road Baths, which is still there but it's been upgraded and modernised since then. They used to have what they called slipper baths there. We used to go there as it was only just around the corner from where we lived. They were only ordinary baths, but they called them slipper baths, I don't know why. When you see photographs or drawings in books of the old baths, they were high up at one end low at the other. And they were the original slipper baths. They were only ordinary baths at Boundary Road, but they called them slipper baths.

Beat Dingsdale

May Days and Walking Days

We used to make tents from bits of rags, and then we used to have May Queens. Every

Agnes Bacon's children enjoying a day at Sutton park, 1962.

May you'd get a group and one would be the May Queen, and there'd be two attendants, and everyone would be dressed in fancy dress. We used to go around the streets, and people would give us money, and when you got back to the house, your parents would have a tea ready – cakes, jellies, and things like that. This happened every May. There was a lot of 'falling-out'. One lad used to be dressed as Robin Hood – they joined in as well. On Whit Sunday at St Peter & Paul's it was the big affair of the year – everybody got new clothes. They did the maypole and the Morris Dancing, and they used to stop outside of Carr Mill Hotel and do a Morris Dance show for the public. When you were a kid you started off in the maypole and then you graduated to the Morris Dancing. We walked all around Haresfinch, and then you'd get a box with a cake in and a

sandwich and a jelly – it was like being back at school at Christmas when you used to have to take your own plate and dish, and you used to have your name stuck on the bottom. They didn't have Sellotape then. Walking day was a really big thing. We all got a new pair of shoes and a new dress – they were really good days.

Roz Moore

There's Little Singing Now

I was born on 8 August 1927, I had a happy childhood, and I'm the youngest of nine. I can remember my mum and dad, especially on Sundays, but on other days during the week, we used to sit around the piano and sing. We used to sing lots of songs that you don't hear at all today. I know quite a few of them myself, and I still sing them. My family knows them as well. But if I go to the club, people talk about all the songs that I know, but all that's dying out now. There's very little singing now. All the songs used to have a good story to them.

Roy Burrows

Mother Married A Moulder

After that mother married a moulder – he was a few years older than she was. He'd joined the forces as a young boy, he wore one of those little pillbox hats and he came back to Haydock, and across the way from where he lived was this young widow with these two children, and he fell in love with her and eventually married her, and they had two boys, and my husband was the younger of those two boys.

Joan Gleave

Walked from St Helens to Atherton

My father was actually a coach driver, and when I was a very young boy I was able to go to most resorts and day-trip places. This was by virtue of my dad being the driver. I was on my own on these coach trips, but always standing up at the front. I used to stand right behind my father, and I watched every move that he made. By the time that I was eight, I could have driven that coach. That's one of my claims to fame – I did actually drive a

The LMS Rose Queen – Panlake Railway Club, 1930.

coach when I was nine years old. It was in the garage and not on the road. My father took the seat back out of the way, and I stood up so that I could get to the pedals. They were great massive pedals in those days. Today the buses have all these button gearboxes, and semi-automatics, but in those days it was the old crash gearbox. My father used to tell me the tale about when he first started driving buses, he worked for LUT, Lancashire United Travel. He started there before the war, and he worked there all through the war, and, although he was based in Atherton, because of the war, he couldn't get any kind of a transfer. It just wasn't on, you had to keep working wherever you were. So he had to walk from St Helens to Atherton on a regular basis in order to do his shifts on the buses. He also

tells the story that when he learnt to drive on the buses, one of the tests was to be able to stop the bus at the bottom of a fairly steep hill, similar to Cropper's Hill here in St Helens, without using either the brakes or the clutch. It sounds impossible, and I don't think that many of today's modern drivers would be able to do it, but you had to be able to do it then, in order to get to drive a bus.

Vincent Woodward

We Were All in the YHA

We used to enjoy trips out, and when we went to Newton-le-Willows – it's all built-up now – we used to go on our bikes. When I got a bit older, and I learned how to ride a bike, half a dozen of us ganged together and joined the YHA. In the late forties we were all in the Youth Hostel Association, and we used to go all over North Wales. Some of the people I used to go with are abroad now, and two or three of them have died. We went in the school holidays, and it was all open country then. You'd go for about three or four miles before a car passed you. We used to pedal away on our bikes – there were no traffic lights, not like there is now, because there were no cars! There were more black Fords on the road than anything else. Apart from them, there was nothing. When we first started travelling, the East Lancs Road had just been opened, and it was empty. You could go for miles without seeing a thing – you might see a car. You might see an odd car or an odd van now and again, but it was mostly bikes, or people walking alongside of the road.

Don Thornley

The home of Isaac Ashton – undertaker, blacksmith and cab driver.

A Crust with Treacle on it

When I went to my Grandma's, she always used to give me a crust with treacle on. That was good for my chest, it was good for colds, etc. We didn't bother whether there was any butter or margarine; it was just a crust with treacle on.

Tommy Dingsdale

Jump Over the Old Middens

It was very rare that my mother lost her temper with me, but there was one day – I'd been a devil on this day for some reason – and, at the bottom of the yards then there was the old middens, as they were called then. They had ashes in and whatever, and I could jump on the midden and over into the back entry, and my mother came chasing me out through the back kitchen and she had the yard brush. She let it go like a javelin, and it whistled past me! As I jumped into the back entry there was an old lady coming up and she insisted that I would finish up on the gallows!

Ken Dale

The Syrup of Figs!

When we lived there, my mother used to bath me at seven o'clock on a Saturday night, and she used to have Palace of Variety on the radio, and she'd always be singing as she was bathing me. After that I used to have a dose of Syrup of Figs and I detested it. The motto then was 'If you feed well, keep your bowels open, then you'd catch no harm'. There was no running to the doctors like they do today. My mother used to pay insurance for the doctors. All the club men used to come on a Friday night – insurance, clothing, doctor, etc. But that Syrup of Figs – I can still taste it today! Sometimes I used to get a choice, it was either that or a chocolate laxative. My grandfather used to have Sennapods. I wanted Sennapods, but my mum wouldn't let me have then for some reason.

Tom Gornall

Mother's Best Scissors

We had a holiday once a year to Anglesey in a boarding house. There were no computers! My daughter speaks to me and tells me that she's having a good time, but it's nothing – it's all about money. We didn't have any money – we didn't get to spend. We used to collect peelings for the pigs on the farm if you wanted money – the farm at Moss Bank. I remember my brother collected them. He stored them in my mother's brick shed. He then forgot about them, and when my mother went in one day – well, you've never seen anything like it. There were flies everywhere! My brother did all kinds of things. One time when the rag and bone man came around, he swopped my mothers best scissors (she was a dressmaker) for a balloon! They were her best cutting-out scissors. He sold his jumpers for a donkey-stone.

Roz Moore

Sunday Night Sod Raids

On Sunday nights we used to have 'sod raids'. We used to pull sods of earth up –

Field day procession passing by the Old Red Lion pub in Robins Lane.

weeds and soil, and then we would wet it and throw it at the opposition! They'd come up to Thatto Heath from Nutgrove or somewhere like that, and we'd have a belting time. After the raid it was all over and forgotten.

Derek Gittins

To Own a Car!

I suppose as kids we did all of the usual things, we played out in the streets, because, as I say, there wasn't that much traffic. I can only think of two people that actually had cars within, say, a third of a mile of where I lived. One of them was a manager at Pilkington's, and the other was a lady who

collected cash for Stirlers, and she had a car. It was like a dreamland, we could never aspire to owning a car.

Vincent Woodward

The Big Rambling Farmhouse

When I was a girl we lived in a big rambling farmhouse in Rainhill, my father was a farmer and then I went on to marry a farmer. After I got married to Tom Green we went to live at Knowsley, and then we moved to Rainford. I had one brother, who was older than me, and he has a farm over Manchester way, and he's still there.

Mary Green

Everything Was 'On Strap'

We lived in a two-up, two-down house, and we had two big beds in each room, and I used to sleep at the bottom of my mum's bed, because I was the baby. Even as I got bigger I still slept at the bottom of their bed. In the back room there was two beds, the girls were at one end, and the boys at the other. The room was filled with beds. On a Saturday night my mum used to go to the market and she'd bring home a bag of broken chocolates. They were only about threepence. At the end of the market on a Saturday you got things for coppers – everything came in a brown bag. I remember those days. My mum was in the Co-op, everybody was in the Co-op then. She had a big wooden cupboard in the pantry, and she had bread, sugar, tea that she was selling – but it was stolen from the Co-op. People used to go to her. They used to call my mum Mrs Glover, although her married name was Cottington. I don't know why she was called Mrs Glover, but my dad used to have stepbrothers called Glover. People used to come for a quarter of tea or a packet of sugar – it was in blue pound bags then. She also had bacon, but they had no fridges then. She used to keep it on a slab in the pantry. Everything was on 'strap', nothing was paid for. Every so often you did get something!

Josie Beard

A Railway Rose Queen crowning in the early 1930s.

Boys dressed ready for their first communion, 1958.

Home Guard Parties

I grew up in a two-up, two-down house. There was a Yorkshire range, and everything was cooked on the fire. There was a brick warming in the oven to warm the bed. This was put in the bed with a towel wrapped around it. After that we got a bit posh, and we got one of these mug things with a screw top. During the war years my dad was in the Home Guard – he was down the pits, so he was excluded, except for the Home Guard duties. I can remember going to the Home Guard parties in Mill Street, they had a conjuror. Not only that, there was stuff there that you would never normally see – they'd worked it so that there was some good stuff for the kids to have. The other main thing that I remember is that you couldn't get blankets and things like that, so I used to end up with my dad's Home Guard great coat on my bed.

Tom Gornall

On Holiday by Coach

Going to Anglesey by coach was a highlight. It was as much of a holiday as the holiday itself was. Going on the coach there was great. We stayed at this boarding house and it was wonderful because that was the only time that we were ever allowed pop with our meal – usually it was water. We used to get on to this charabanc with all of our cases. I loved it because we got new clothes for the holiday. The rest of the year we made do, but for holidays we got a new outfit. We used to go every year from the time that I was about five until I was fourteen, and then we went to Scarborough, and that was on a coach as well. My dad couldn't drive – nobody could drive, and even if they could they couldn't have afforded a car. The trip in the old charabanc really was a highlight – you still see some today, but they're called nostalgia buses now. Going abroad was never thought of.

Roz Moore

We Got A Works House

We had plots and we kept chickens. We grew our own vegetables. I was seven before we got our own house. There was just me and my brother, and we moved up to Thatto Heath. That was our first council house, and I was there from the time that I was seven up until I was eleven. At eleven we got a works house, but it wasn't as good as the council house to be honest. We came back to mind my grandfather who was a retired sergeant major. He was dying of cancer and my mother nursed him.

Agnes Bacon

Sunday School Teacher

I used to go to church regularly and eventually I became a Sunday School teacher. I had small children, and tried to teach them the right way of life. I started

Joan and Bert Gleave with their daughter Claire and newly-born son, Andrew, early 1950s.

to be a Sunday school teacher when I was about eleven and I carried on until I was about eighteen.

Mary Green

Salvation Army Soup

I was going to the Salvation Army, and we went for our bowl of soup, and we used to sing a few hymns, and that was because some of my friends had brothers and they always used to go there. That was my start in life as a Christian – is was a little bit dicey to say a Christian, by just going to the Salvation Army for the soup and the hymns! I then moved over to the Methodist Mission in Balmer Street. I could play football and cricket there. It was a part of Christianity. Finally I went to Ravenhead – that's where I got married. I know the vicar there and I joke with him and say that I've forgiven him since!

Tommy Dingsdale

English Electric Locomotives

I worked at the Vulcan. I didn't work much because of my health, but when I did work, I worked at the Vulcan Foundry in Newton-le-Willows, where they built the locos – the steam locos. After that they went on to these Deltics, and then English Electric took it over, and the firm that's got it at the moment, they took it over. They only build electrical parts there now. When I first started there in the early fifties they were still building steam locos, and I was helping out in the stores. That's the job that I got, and it was interesting work. When you had a break, you could have a walk around the factory, and see these locos starting small and then see the finished product. A few times when I went out into the yard there'd be an engine driver, and they'd be running the engine on the yard to test them before they put them on the line. On a few times, if you were walking on the yard, they'd ask you where you were going. I was only going from one shop to another in the factory, and they'd give me a lift on the footplate. They were exporting some of them to India. When you see all these films on BBC and ITV, these old films, with thousands of people piled up on them, standing all over the place, if you could see the nameplate on those locos – even today – you'd see that it said English Electric Locomotives, Newton-le-Willows, Lancashire, England. Remember that this was before Merseyside came on the scene. I still think of myself as a Lancastrian. Whenever anybody writes to me I always reply putting St Helens, Lancashire, although it's St Helens, Merseyside officially.

Don Thornley

Hopscotch and Lampo

We used to play hopscotch, and 'lampo'. That was a game where there were two teams at opposite ends of the street. After a shout of, 1-2-3, you had to try and get to the other end of the street whilst trying to stop kids from the other team getting to what had been your end of the street. There were lots of silly games, like treasure hunt or just knocking on doors and running off. We never thought that that was bad. Whenever we went to see a

Cross country runners from St Helens taking part in a military meeting at Aldershot, 1914.

film, all the games that we played the following week took their theme from the film – like, if we went to see a cowboy film, then we played cowboys all that week.

Roz Moore

Bottle-Shaped Ovens

We used to go over where the teapot works is. It wasn't too far from Greengate brick works. They had these bottle-shaped ovens, and I used to love going on there to see what I could find. It was amazing just what you could find. I used to find cups that hadn't been fired properly and things like that. It was marvellous to us, just like treasure trove. My mam used to think that I pinched it, but I never did – I just went in and took it!

Derek Gittins

Taylor Park

The other big park was called the Taylor Park. I've already mentioned one grandma that lived opposite Grange Park, well, I had another grandma who lived along Bretherton Road which is by Toll Bar. So again, it was an easy hop, skip and a jump across the road. I was a regular visitor to the playground when I was a kid and also to Taylor Park. Taylor Park also had the attraction of the lakes. It had the big lake, the big boating lake, and the small paddling pool. Unfortunately, even in those days, there was some vandalism. By the time that I was about seven, it was rather dangerous to go paddling in this pool unless you'd got shoes on of some kind. There was broken glass and other things in the lake, but the rest of the park was kept up. They had park keepers in those days, and if you got up to any mischief then, like myself, you got a clip around the ear. There were two big playing fields there, and on an average Sunday – especially in the summer – there were, literally, thousands of people there. The last time I went to Taylor Park, which was only about three years ago, I don't think that I saw more than fifty or sixty people in the whole of the park, and it's a big area. Unfortunately, many of the people that I did see were 'undesirables', really.

Vincent Woodward

'I'll Have That One'

I was born in St Helens and I can remember living in 32 Henry Street – I was about four or five. I had a grandma, and my mother had two children older than me by her first husband, and she married a young man and had a little girl, she was three months pregnant, and her husband died in the big flu epidemic. The First World War came, and different ones came back from the forces, and my father, whose name was Roberts, he was one of five children who lived up Prescot Road. Whilst they were all in the forces, both their mum and dad died within a week of each other in the flu epidemic – the same flu epidemic that my mother's first husband died in. There were a lot of people that died in that flu epidemic. So, when my father came back from the forces there was no home to go to, because both of his parents had died. But, his elder sister lived next door to this young widow who had these two little children. He fell in love with her, and then married her. From there they moved to a bit bigger house because, as I say, there was one or two more

The First Communion Procession, 1960.

46

children coming along. They moved to Rigby Street.

I went to Windle Pilkington School, that was near to Beechams. My older brother went there, I went there, and my younger sister also went there. One day I came home from school and there was a strange lady playing the piano – we always had the piano. Quite a severe lady, with her hair tied back. She said, 'You'd better all go upstairs', and my mum was in bed with a new baby – a little boy whom she called Harold. When we came down my dad told us that this lady was our Aunty Margaret – she was my dad's sister. Before she went home, they lined us all up. There was Nancy and Tom who were the children by her first husband, there was Jack who's eighteen months older than me, Marjorie and me. So, we lined up and Marjorie started crying. I just stood there I wasn't bothered, and Jack said that he wasn't going, so she said, 'I'll have that one". She didn't even know my name! So, I put my hat and coat on and she got hold of my hand. We went to Victoria Square and we got on a bus, and she took me to where she lived which was Earlestown. It was near to the Market Square, and it was a big shop with a step. I can remember looking at that shop, and on the step was what I thought was the tallest man that I'd ever seen. He had a big white coat on and a shock of black hair. She told me that that was Uncle Harold. I was a good girl and I did what I was told. I'd been used to sleeping three in a bed, because at my house there was my mum and dad, now the new baby, Nancy, Tom, Jack and Marjorie, my mother's brother who was gassed in the First World War and her father who was an elderly gentleman. So, I suppose that's why they were glad for one to be away for the weekend, because that's what it was for. There were a lot to look after.

They were very kind to me and they gave me a doll, a lovely big doll. The little girl from around the corner came to play with me. The next day she came round again and asked if I could come out to play. With being in the shopping area, you only had to go around the corner and the Town Hall was there. There was another girl called Audrey Martindale. The Town Hall side door had marble steps up, so they took me to these steps and we were playing 'house', and the little girl said that she would mind the baby whilst I did the cooking. I gave her the doll and she promptly dropped it! It was smashed – I was frightened to death to go back, but I had to go. I was told that I'd never get another doll like that. They did buy me another one, but it was a rag doll with a rag body and just a little face. They were kind to me, but they never sent me home! After about ten days, a gentleman called and asked if there was a child in the house called Joan Roberts and my aunt said, 'Yes'. They said that it had been reported that I hadn't been going to school. She got hold of my hand, and, as we lived next door to the district school, she went to see the headmaster. Mr Spurr was the headmaster, he was a nice man. I was introduced to him, so he put me in a class and that was it. She never sent me home! I never went back to live with my family – I was six at the time. I was a happy little girl. I came home from school no problem, and we had a back yard then with the shop, and a sitting room with a large window. I looked through the window, and there was a lady sat in the yard with a boy in a chair who wasn't very well. She was a lovely looking lady with black hair, and I asked my aunty who it was. She told me that it was my mother, and I didn't know it was my real mother! My mother must have felt that she wanted to come and see me. They

Iris Briscoe with two of her children at a family wedding.

The procession for First Communion at Lowe House church.

were kind to me there, and I was good for them. But, I could never do it to a child of mine, it's just not fair. I used to daydream, and think how lovely it must be to be brought up with brothers and sisters, and I had been brought up as an only child. I used to be put on the bus, because all of the bus drivers used to know me because they all came into our shop – we sold sweets, fizzy drinks and cigarettes. The other part was a gent's hairdresser. My aunt used to ask the drivers to see me off at Victoria Square in St Helens and they'd always arrange for somebody to be there to meet me. I started to go home and see my brothers and sisters who I hadn't seen, and also my mum and dad. When I was about nine I knew that I wanted to go home – I must have been feeling home sick. The little girl around the corner wasn't as old as me, so I said to her that I was going to see my mother and father. She said that she wanted to go with me. We walked all the way from Earlestown to St Helens. I knew the way I was going – up Market Street, down the Common, over the canal, through Newton Road Park to Finger Post. On the way past Victoria Square, I knew where Rigby Street was. I just knocked on the front door – I forget who opened the door. Somebody shouted, 'Who is it?' and whomever it was who answered just said that it was 'our Joan'. I walked all the way – it must have been about eight miles. I got pulled over the coals for that. I just needed to go. My aunt came and took me back. I still believe that I should have been allowed to stop at home, but then I couldn't. When I was old enough to say that I wanted to go back, I couldn't for shame leave my aunt and uncle because they'd been so good to me. They didn't have any children.

Joan Gleave

The Bobby Told My Mother

When I was little I used to get into trouble from time to time. We used to throw 'sods', which were just lumps of turf. It was nothing like they do today with knives and fighting. My grandma used to live in Parliament Street, but I was born in Elephant Lane, but because my mum spent all day Monday washing, all day Tuesday ironing – because there were no electric irons, and all day Wednesday was cleaning up the stairs etc, so I used to go to my grandmother's quite a lot. I was actually fighting with my Parliament Street pals against the ones where I lived in Elephant Lane, and I was pretty fast then as I played a lot of sport. The bobby chased us on his push-bike, and we were going round this block, and I was that fast that I caught him up! Bobby Glover knew everybody, and he had his own house with a sign over the top declaring that it was also a police station. You could go to the policeman anytime, but now you can't get hold of a policeman. There was more discipline then. We were terrified when he threatened to tell our mother – you couldn't get a worse punishment. Sometimes you wouldn't be doing anything as such, except being sat on the pavement. I was made to go and pile up all of the 'sods'. My mother's face was going redder and redder when the policeman accompanied me home. He said that he'd punished me by making me pick up all of the 'sods'. He left the final punishment with my mother! I was wishing that I'd have been put in the lock-up! I was chastised and had to take my punishment. It was a different world then.

Tommy Dingsdale

49

My Dad Was a Bricklayer

My dad was a journeyman bricklayer, and my first memories of him was coming home with three pounds ten – that's three pounds and fifty pence in today's money. We'd nothing, but we were happy! I remember my dad and his brothers, Uncle Dick and Uncle George making a biplane for me, a wind up one with elastic bands. The first time I took it out it went into the brook! My dad wasn't too pleased, and said that he wouldn't make me any more.

Derek Gittins

I Hated the Three Stooges

On a Saturday there was a matinee. I hated the Three Stooges. They frightened me because they used to hit one another and I didn't like that. My dad often used to ask my sister, who was a bit older than me, to take me to the pictures. She always asked me if I really wanted to go, because she didn't really want to take me. I always asked if the Three Stooges were on, and she always said that they were – so I wouldn't go. I only found out years later that they weren't on! There used to be a sing-song before the big picture started, and there was a lady who used to stand at the front conducting, and if you didn't sing then you'd get a crack on the head. Of course there were no televisions then, and I remember the school taking us to the Capital to see the Coronation – it was wonderful and in colour! The days were so full.

Roz Moore

Mum Had Fourteen

My mum had fourteen kiddies and I was the youngest – she reared ten. All the lads worked at Pilkingtons, the girls worked at the BI at Prescot. We all had a job, we had to do. When we were younger, there was a terrible accident. We used to play up in the sandbeds at the Kimicks as they called them in the centre of town. One of the hollows that we used to play in collapsed, and there was all kiddies in it. They were all buried. One or two did get out. I was a bit too young and my mother wouldn't let me go. Two of my brothers were already there, twins, our Tom and our John. We were out of our minds because we knew that they were playing on the sandbeds. Anyway, the long and the short of it is that they were alright, thank God.

Josie Beard

I Saw Mum Twice a Week

I lived in my grandparent's house, I don't really know why. When I went to live with my grandparents, my own parents lived only about thirty or forty yards away, and then they moved on, and they finished up having seven more children, and I stayed with my grandparents on my own. My father got killed when he came back from Dunkirk. We never saw him. He came home one day from the Maginot Line, and then they went back and the Germans overtook them. He was missing for five days at Dunkirk, and then he got home to Scotland. He was due to come home on the Saturday, but he came home in a coffin. He was killed up in Scotland. My mum brought those seven children up during the war, and then after

Lining up to make their first communion.

the war they all got married off, and then she died.

I used to go and see my mother twice a week, on a Friday and on a Sunday.

Bill Barrow

Jessie, Ellen and George Douglas – Agnes Bacon's sisters and brother.

CHAPTER 3
At School

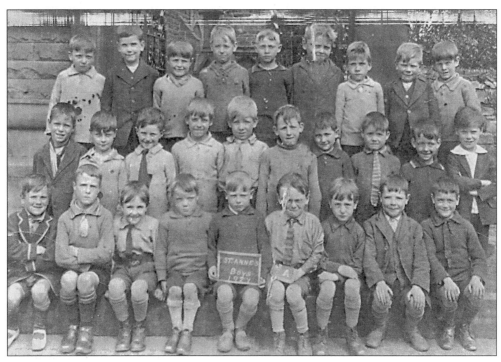

As the notice proudly proclaims – St Anne's Boys 1927.

St Teresa's School

I went to St Teresa's School, St Teresa's, New Town. I seem to remember that I started school at the age of four, and then it had to be put back a bit because war broke out. One has vague recollections – it's funny how propaganda must get to young people – I've been in the schoolyard chanting with other young kids, 'We want war; we want war...' We didn't realise what we were saying. It's only looking back that you realise that it was a horrible thing to want. St Teresa's was quite a good school; it was like all the other schools around there. It was the local Catholic school. It catered for youngsters from the age of five right through to, I suppose, it was fourteen in those days, and then it went up to fifteen. I was lucky in the sense that I passed the scholarship, which, at that stage, quite a number of people passed from St Teresa's because it had a good reputation, in being able, I suppose, prepare youngsters for taking the scholarship. I went to what was then called the Catholic Grammar School, before it had a name change and became West Park. I don't think that people at that stage knew that West Park was West Park, but it's a rather classier address now on your address in St Helens – with apologies to anyone who happens to live in West Park.

Brian Coxhead

His Cane Rapped the Desk

At school we had a very strict headmaster, and I didn't like school in my younger days. The only time that I liked school was when I stayed on until I was fifteen. I was in the first group that stayed on until we were fifteen. That was my best year at school. We had little Mr Kidd, Billy Kidd, and he'd been a sergeant major in the army. I think that he thought that he was still in the army. He used to have a cane with a handle over his arm, and that was his 'friend'. When they were short of teachers he'd take us sometimes, and he'd explain a question or a problem, whatever it was, just the once, and then he'd come down the line and his cane would rap on your desk, and he'd demand an answer. You had to stand up and explain the answer – I was terrified. My brother liked this approach. I had one brother and two sisters, Muriel the eldest, Margaret the youngest, and my brother, Bernard, two years older than me.

Jean Dale

Had to Leave and Get a Job

I went to Thatto Heath School. I wasn't all that good at school, but I was good at sports, so I captained the school at cricket, I captained them at rugby and I was vice captain of the soccer team. In fact, I got my leg broken playing rugby at school which threw me back a bit, so I could never climb up the ladder because I had to leave school. And also, with people being poor, you had to leave school and get a job straight away, and put something back into the coffers, because I had two sisters who were both younger than me.

Tommy Dingsdale

Back to Thatto Heath School

I remember school being divided, with boys on one side and girls on the other. When you went out of the juniors and into the seniors, there was a wall across, so you couldn't get back into the juniors. I was up there a few weeks ago, because they're going to make a Hall of Fame. I had a portrait painted, as I was the president of the Art Centre, although I'm not an artist myself. One of my friends asked me if I'd like to be president, so they painted my portrait, and it was unveiled by Bishop David Shepherd and his wife Grace. So this will be installed as the first one in the school, so I'm going back to Thatto Heath School and doing this thing, because I think that the kids of today are like me. They think that anything is beyond them, so it's just to prove to them that going to Thatto heath School, you can still attain something.

St Anne's girls, c. 1930.

I'm no different from them, and I think that a lot of it is got by just being in the right place at the right time.

Tommy Dingsdale

Clogs for School

I remember going to school when it was snowing. We used to have a lot of snow then. I went to Windle Hurst first – which is still there today, and then I went to Rivington Road School. Getting from Seddon Street to school then, there were no cars or buses – you had to walk in the early '40s when the war was on. We walked along in the snow, starting off as being 4ft 6in tall, and by the time that you got to Rivington Road you were well over 5ft, because of the snow that collected under your clogs. Everyone used to wear clogs for school, as we couldn't afford shoes. Clogs were a very warm foot article. It didn't matter whether there were irons under the clogs or rubbers, the snow still collected underneath. Mr Penrose from St Helens was the headmaster – he only died recently. He was connected with St Helens Football Club.

Ken Dale

A Hiding for Nothing!

I was born in 1919, exactly twelve months after the war finished. I always remember my school days, how times have changed since those days. My parents, the same as a lot of other parents, were very strict. If you did anything wrong outside of the home – for instance, if you did something at school and

54

you got the cane, when you came home and told your parents then you'd get a good hiding, because of that! We used to respect teachers, police – anybody in authority. The way we were brought up carried us through the years. Your attitude to other people was entirely different to what the youngsters have now. I remember one time, I must have only been about eleven or twelve, and there used to be about five or six of us, and we went carol singing. We went up Greenfield Road, and out by there was a small cycle shop. As we got there, two lads came towards us – they were brought up in the next street to us – so we stopped talking for a while. After that we went on our way. The following afternoon, the police came to the school and called us out and took us to the Town Hall where the police station used to be in those days. They questioned us individually. It seemed that a cycle lamp had been stolen from outside of this shop. The consequence was, when I got home I was late. My father asked where I'd been, so I told him – I got a really good hiding! The following day at school, the police came and called us out, and then apologised – but we'd had this good hiding!

Henry Atherton

Tried to Teach Us Latin

I went to Ravenhead. I enjoyed school days. We started off in what was called the babies class, and then you moved up, and you were finished by the time that you were fourteen. A teacher used to have you for a whole year, there was no change in teachers or anything like that. She taught you everything. There was one teacher who even tried to teach us Latin, but it was hopeless! Schooldays were

very easy-come, easy-go. Looking back on it now, we had a sergeant major. He used to line us all up to come into the school, it was army-fashion. You did a right turn and then you marched in. The first line would file into the class, and then the rest. As you marched in up the pathway, with Standard 6 on one side and Standard 7 on the other – they had their own rooms – in front of you, there was a cane hung on the wall. There was also a map of the world on the wall. There were all little bits in red – they were ours! As for reading – we had Kipling, Shakespeare and the Bible. It was a church school, and the vicar used to come around every so often looking for choirboys. You used to have to stand up and try to sing. He got some, and they used to have a fair choir. We didn't do that much sport from what I can recall, but I do remember playing in a rugby team on the Saints as a curtain raiser. I think that it was called the Ellison Cup.

Douglas Ashton

We Had Nuns As the Headmistresses

I went to Lowe House School at the bottom of Duke Street, and we had nuns as headmistresses, and believe you me, they were sadists – some of them – that's the only word I can use to describe them. I enjoyed my school days though. When I look at the school now, long after I've left, it looks ever so small, but it always seemed very big to me. We used to have to walk to the swimming baths, and walk for our dinner to Gerrard's Hall School – not like now, were it's all laid on.

Roz Moore

Who Remembers Miss Pearce?

The earliest memory that I can put a date to is when I started school, but I think that I have memories from before that, but nothing that I can put a date to. The war was on, it was in 1942 that I started school and the windows were sandbagged. Eventually they took the sandbags down, and put brick walls in front. The war ended before we saw daylight through the windows – that was a traumatic event. I went to Thatto Heath Council School. My sister went ten years before me, and now my granddaughter's there. They've messed it about a bit since my time, there are a lot of extensions and they've changed the whole environment – some for the better, and yet, you can still like the way that things were. Schools are a lot different now, they seem to have different approaches. When I first

started there, there was no playschool or preparatory school, or anything like that. You started at five, and you were in – straight away – to schooling. You had to go to bed in the afternoon, I still puzzle about what their reason for that was, because I was always made to go to bed early anyway. Perhaps it was for the people who never put their children to bed – I just couldn't say what the reasoning behind that was. In those days you couldn't please yourselves, you were told to do that, and do that you did. So that's my earliest recollection. My first recollection was my first teacher, she was Miss Pickerskill, and she had us all sat cross-legged on the concrete floor. I can still see that very vividly. When I think back, those council schools were exceptionally good in those days. As you develop and you go from the infants to the juniors as you did then, I was never chastised in any hard way,

Children from Sutton National School with teacher Miss Golding and headmaster Frank Plews.

St Anne's girls in the 1950s.

other than by one teacher who was notorious at the time. She slapped me, and it was the only time that I was ever reprimanded. I think that this particular teacher was well known for it. I can't remember what it was for, but her name was Miss Pearce and she lived in Leslie Road. There must be a lot of people in St Helens that still remember Miss Pearce.

Then I moved up to the secondary modern as it was called then. I should have gone to Cowley, but that wasn't to be. In those days, if you went to a grammar school, then you needed a uniform, and you needed a lot of money for that – there'd been a change in family circumstances, so I went to the secondary modern. Consequently, I found myself at the top of the class in most

subjects – apart from maths, where I used to be second or third or something like that. By the time I was in the third year I just wanted to leave school – I'd had enough of this studious business! I left school and I went looking for a job for the next six months.

Tom Gornall

A Lover of Cricket

My parents were intending to move house – they weren't terribly happy with my schooling at St Austin's. I think the school's greatest achievements were for playing rugby, and not very much on the academic side of things. My parents wanted me to go to a better school, and they tried to move house to the Denton's Green area. Because they were going to move house there, they managed to get me a place at Windleshaw, which was actually St Thomas of Canterbury. The house move fell through, but I kept the place at the school. Having got there, I had to be demoted as it were. I thought that I should have been in Standard 4, but the standard of education at St Thomas of Canterbury was so much higher, that I was really only on a level of two classes down. I had to accept that, but I was very disappointed as I thought that I was quite clever! Eventually I got to West Park – the grammar school, but I did it on the 13 plus, although I did quite well in the 11 plus. It seems that unlike the GCSE and similar exams, there isn't a pass mark as such, it's just a question of how many places are available at the schools. I always seemed to be one year behind in my education. I did reasonably well at school. I mentioned before that I was a lover of cricket, a very avid cricketer by this stage, and cricket took over my mind when it should have been Maths and Chemistry. My actual GCE's were not that brilliant – I got 4, but that was over a two-year period. Maths I never had a problem with – I got a credit in Maths. In the two years I got History, Geography and English Language – just about!

Vincent Woodward

In 1986 Lady Pilkington opened the Gerards Lane Adventure Playground.

The Class of '65 at Grange Park School.

Girls Got Caned on the Legs

I used to go to Parish Church School; it was in Charles Street down Pocket Nook Street. It's at the bottom of Standish Street – there's Parish Church and there's Holy Cross School. I used to go to Parish Church School, but I don't remember much about when I went to school. All I remember was that we had a Mr Yates and if you wasn't paying attention he used to sling the chalk or the board duster at you! We used to get caned on the legs. If you did anything that you needed punishing for, then you got caned on the legs. Mr Yates used to cane the girls on their legs, but the boys used to get it on their hands and on their bums, but the girls used to get it on the bottom of their legs. If you went to school

and got caned, when you got home and told your mum that you didn't like going to that school – when you said that you'd been caned, then you'd get another crack at home for doing something wrong! There were about thirty or so pupils in any class, and you only had one teacher who used to take you for everything – arithmetic, history and so on, and you still got homework, and if you hadn't finished it then you'd get a crack the next morning! If you were playing in the schoolyard with the boys then you got caned, because this was one of the things that you shouldn't be doing. You didn't get caned for nothing, it was always for something that you shouldn't be doing.

Iris Briscoe

Everyone seems to be smiling here!

The 'Boardy Men' Are Coming

If the men were coming round to mend the road, and children would often play 'wag'. I was mesmerised with the steamroller. The men had this little portable cabin, and they carried it about with them so that they had somewhere to drink their tea. One day I was invited in to have a cup of tea, and before I knew where I was, instead of spending half an hour with them, I was spending half a day with them! I used to go home and my parents would ask me how school had gone that day. They would gradually draw everything out of me, and then they would confront me and suggest that I

hadn't been to school that day! I made excuses about being interested in what the workmen were doing. Whenever the people from the truancy board came around, the men would tell me to keep down as the 'boardy men' were coming. I was into road building in a big way!

Ken Dale

You Can't Go Back

After St Austin's I went to Grange Park Senior Boys School. It was alright, but I went for the gym, because we had no gymnasium in the Catholic school. Everything cost the earth – well, we thought that it cost the earth but you used to get a pile of toffees for two pence! They were good times and I look back on them with yearnings – but you never can go back.

Derek Gittins

The Best Trainers?

We used to get the cane – but it didn't do me any harm. If your parent came down to complain you would be mortified. But, if I'd have gone home and said that I'd been caned at school today, then I'd have just got another one. But they were happy days. Nobody bothered about who had the best trainers.

Roz Moore

I've Still Got The Scar

I remember drinking small bottles of milk from school. I pinched one once, or thought that I was pinching it, and I dropped it. It smashed, so I picked the glass up and some got stuck in my finger – I've still got the scar. I did that when I was throwing the bottle away, so that I wouldn't get caught!

Derek Gittins

Played a Lot of Sport

I wasn't brought up with my own parents, I was brought up by my grandparents. It was as though I was brought up with a silver spoon in my mouth. We had a big family, and they were all working. When the war broke out in '39, I was one of twenty boys in

St Helens who left school in November, instead of going through to the following year. I was just fourteen when I left school. At school I used to do a lot of athletics, cricket, rugby, soccer, swimming, and then my Achilles went, which people know about now, but my ankles went, and it made me flat-footed. Most of my life as a boy, was taken up with sport in St Helens. I used to play a lot of table tennis up to going in the army. I joined the Army Cadet Corps, and I used to play cricket for them. After I got called up, that was it! The rest of my life has been spent in bringing my four kids up.

Bill Barrow

Got Picked On At School

I always got picked on at school. I went to school on this particular day, and I had a white shirt on – as it happens, my dad had been to the same school years before – and the headmaster, who was the same guy as when my dad had been there, must have had something against me. He started to prod me with a pencil. I can still remember running out of school with blood all over my shirt. My dad went up to the school and sorted him out! I left school when I was sixteen.

John Lee

Omnia Perficery Portest

I went to Parr Central School, and the headmaster there was a chap called Jack Houghton, and it was the only school that I know had a motto. There was a school motto and a school song. The motto was

Children from St Austin's School, Thatto Heath, c. 1920.

Omnia Perficery Portest. I think that it's
Latin, and it means – It can be done. The
song is as follows:

> In days when work seemed very hard
> When all you did earned scant reward
> You still must try your level best
> Omnia Perficery Portest.

I liked school. I wasn't bad at maths, history,
geography and English. I just enjoyed
school.

Roy Burrows

CHAPTER 4
St Helens At Work

The northside of St Helens Central Station.

Herding the Cows

When I was round about the age of eleven, I was very interested in the cattle farm at the top of our road, which was Seddon Street. It leads into Hard Lane where Skippers is now. There was a farm there called Cabbage Hall Farm, Foster's Cabbage Hall Farm. We used to go down to Moss Bank, where the Moss Bank public house is now, but that was Moss Bank Station then. We used to wait for the cattle trucks coming in from Wales and

Scotland. They used to come off, and we used to take them to Cabbage Hall Farm, for say a week or a fortnight to fatten up off the pastures there, and then we used to take them, all by road, right down into St Helens and to the abattoir. We used to have to pass a lot of cross streets, but there wasn't quite the same traffic as there is now. We used to pick a leader from the farm when they came down every morning and night to drink at the big pond, just where the Windle Hotel is now. We'd pick one out, and then we'd

The newly-built cooling towers at Bold power station in the 1950s.

Members of Sutton Historic Society – down the mines.

round them up, usually on a Thursday, and then herd them all down. We came to Hard Lane and then into Seddon Street where I lived. Everyone had their own job, we knew where all the crossroads were, and as they all passed you at that particular crossroads, then you'd be the next to run down to the next on. This went on all the way through to the abattoir. There was a furniture shop at the bottom of North Road which was called Sarah Ann Taylor's and, unfortunately, one day, a cow got into the shop! There was some good furniture in the shop, and some of these cows had pretty big horns. The damage was done before we managed to get it out again. I'm sure that they paid some recompense for all the damage that was done. Out of all the sorties we did with these cattle, it was the one and only mistake I can remember. I had a very weak chest and I was always off school. The doctor said that I should work on a farm when I left school. It was great working on the farm. I used to look forward going down to Moss Bank station to get the cows off the cattle trucks there and keep them milling round – just like they do in cowboy films now. When we were ready to go, we'd give them a quick slap up the back, and they used to go.

Ken Dale

Working at Tootal's

I left at fifteen and went to work at Tootal's – it was Tootal's then. They made dressing gowns, scarfs, and they had a weaving place there. I started at fifteen. I left school on the Friday and started – it was Bank holiday – on the Tuesday. There was no choice really; you just went there. We started at half past seven and worked through till half past five and quarter to six on Thursday, with half an hour for lunch. But, because we were only fifteen and we weren't really allowed to

Steaming towards St Helens junction, 1980.

Sutton Oak Sheeting Sheds – originally built by the St Helens Railway Company as their engine sheds.

work that many hours, we were sent to college. We used to go to college one day a week. We used to go for English in the morning, and then it was pottery in the afternoon. I worked there for twelve and a half years before I had the children.

Roz Moore

A Job in the Office

I went to Nevin's, a grocer's shop, and I was also going to night school. Then I went to live with my aunty in Leyland for a couple of years and I worked in a dyer and finishers. The material used to come in, in the grey as they called it, and it used to go out like satin. I used to be on the inspection table. I eventually

passed the exams for the shorthand and typing and I came back home. During the war I worked at the BI and I was working on the shop floor drilling – drilling bomb tails, because there was a war on! The weather we used to get then, it was nothing to walk from Thatto Heath through to Prescot, because of the ice and fog which we don't get now. In summer we used to change into dresses on Easter Sunday, and then, when it got towards winter, we were digging ourselves out of the houses. We don't do that today. Anyway, going back. I wrote in for my wages once because I hurt my foot, and they asked me if I'd like a job in the office because of my writing. We were getting a 100 per cent bonus at the time which we thought was very good – it was about £5 or £6 a week. I went in the office, got married, had the children and then went back to the BI. I ended up being the secretary to two managers and supervisor of the typing pool. I hadn't seen them all for twenty-two years and then one of them rang me up the other day and told me that they were having a re-union. I walked in the door and they all mobbed me – it was really lovely. I had about fourteen girls working for me – all typists. They thought that I was like a mother to them – they're in their forties now, but I'm in my seventies.

Mary Knox

The Yanks Were Everywhere

It was coming up to wartime. Bert Birkhead had a younger brother Ken who had to go into the forces, so I was asked to go and help him out. There was a lot of work to do where I was – you could serve in the shop until 10 o'clock. We used to be open until all hours, so I was in and out of there like a bottle cork. I went and worked for Bert Birkhead for a while. There was only Bert and an elderly sister who only came in part-time. Of course, when you got to seventeen, you had to decide whether you were going to go into the forces. When you were eighteen you had to go in anyway. I couldn't make my mind up. I had a friend, Joyce, she worked for the Co-Op which was in the next road. She said that she was going in the WRAFs, but I didn't want to go into the forces. I went working at Burtonwood Aerodrome when the RAF had it. I was in the offices doing all the bookkeeping. One day when we went in, the Americans had taken over. The corridors were full of Yanks, just laying there. They'd arrived in the night and they'd just got down to kip. It was like walking the plank – GIs everywhere, thousands of them! Gradually, they took our jobs over, and

then they wanted us to go to Sealand, but I didn't want to go so far away from home. I started to look around, so I went to the job centre, and they needed someone in the offices at the Vulcan. I did wages and income tax there. They sent me to Manchester to be trained.

Joan Gleave

We Used the Pawnshops

We were poor, my father only worked for three days a week. We had to go on 'relief' for the rest of the time. My mother had to go to the 'relief' to keep us. Until we all gradually began to put money in, we went to the pawnshops like other people. We used to go on a Monday morning and then get them out on a Friday afternoon. My grandmother had sons, and she used to pawn their suits on a Monday and then got them back on Friday afternoon. They all worked down the mines. My father worked at Doulton's. He made the pipes. They were moulded in clay, baked in the kiln, and when they came out he used to hold the pipes between his legs and then pour hot tar around it to finish it off. From that he got cancer. He was operated on, but then he lived for a long time after that. When he worked, it was real hard labour. He used to be in a shed with a big fire in, so that they could warm the tar.

Agnes Bacon

Worked at Triplex

I started work at fourteen and I worked at Triplex. I worked there when they were building it – I worked there until long after the war, and then I went to Cowley Hill in the drawing office there. I retired from there. I was there technical clerk there – I had all of the technical business to see to. I had two brothers, but they're dead now. One worked at Pilkington Brothers as a glass cutter, and the other was a painter.

Jack Rimmer

Looked after the Family

My mum died when I was fifteen, so I left school a couple of months before I should have done. I looked after my dad, my brother and my younger sister – my elder sister had got married by this time. I got a part time job at the newsagents on the bottom corner, Wainwrights – I went down there at teatime. It was right opposite to the baths, so you got a lot of customers from the swimming baths. I did service in the Isle of Man for twelve months. I was seventeen, turned eighteen while I was there. It was hard work but I really enjoyed it. We had to meet the 'Scotch' boats at four o'clock in the morning! I've always done that sort of thing. I came home and started at Pilk's canteen, and then I went on to Bold power station – I worked in the canteen there till I had my first child at twenty-four.

Jean Dale

Mary Jane Wells outside her shop in Junction Lane, 1926.

Women workers stacking cut turf so that it can dry in the sun, on the Moss.

Pilkingtons Head Office

I worked in the head office. I used to send the glass over to Ireland, and when I retired the British & Irish Steam Packet Company gave me a holiday in Southern Ireland up to £500. I could take someone with me, so I took my aunt. She was very good when my mum was ill. They took me to the Waterford crystal factory and bought me a bon-bon dish of Waterford crystal, and the haulier that I'd dealt with for twenty-three years bought me a watch, and bought my aunt a gypsy ring. Daniel Barratt his name was, and his wife still carts for Pilkingtons. Every Christmas she still sends me a Christmas present. It was a lovely holiday, and my photograph was in the *Pilkington News* – I've still got it. I'd never met Daniel Barratt, so he met us over in Dublin, took us into a big hotel there, and we had a meal together. We then went on our holiday. We picked the coach up at Bray, and went all round the Ring of Kerry.

Edith Blackmore

A Very Good Glasscutter

Like everyone else, Joe, my eldest brother got a job here at Pilkington's, and a Major Weeks saw him and was talking to him, and he thought that he was better fixed as regards his education, in having a proper job, and he would speak for him at Pilkingtons. So, he got him a job and he was a glasscutter, and he made a very good glasscutter in a very short time. None of us went into Pilkington's. I was growing up, and Mary was growing up. The others got jobs and just drifted away. Mum and dad were left with me and Ann, my younger sister. Mary, the one whose mother had died,

69

The view from Bold power station looking towards St Helens town centre.

she went on to become a dressmaker – she was very clever.

Margaret Sill

Jumped when a Crowd Had Gathered

My mother always told me that my father's downfall was not having a trade, so I did my best to get a trade – and I did! I worked for a firm that used to have their yard and offices in Fenton Street, but it's called Fenton Place now – this area of the town's changed so much. I served my time as a bricklayer. I worked for J. Yearsley & Sons – it's the son of one of them who runs it now. Joseph Yearsley was the founder – I carried on working for them. Life just progressed. I left round about 1964. I've worked on just about every Roman Catholic establishment around. It was a Roman Catholic firm, but I was a 'left-footer'. Most of the lads that they employed were from Lowe House School. In those days there was always talk about 'keep it in the faith'. I puzzled this, because it seems to be bigotry, even in a polite form.

One chap committed suicide. This chap was always the comedian on site. One of has favourite jokes was about being married. He was always very 'tight'. In those days we'd bring a can and share a brew. This chap never seemed to have a brew, and he was always trying to cadge off other people. One day I was informed that he'd committed suicide. I couldn't believe it, and thought that it might be his brother. In those days Thatto Heath was like a village, and everybody knew everybody, but I only knew the people that I'd grown up with and those I'd been to school with. If I wanted to know anything about anybody locally, then I'd ask my mother. She knew most things that were going on. When I think back about this chap, he really was mean. When he used to get on the trolleybus, he just used to look out of the window when the conductor came along. Sometimes I'd be ashamed, and I'd pay for him – he was just that kind of guy. He jumped off the roof of his house. He broke every bone in his body. Apparently, he only jumped because a crowd had gathered and a policeman was coming around.

Tom Gornall

Enjoyed Being in the Army

When I left I was a fitter and turner at Varleys. That's flattened now. First of all I went to Hall and Kelly's, and they used to make bricks. Then, that shut down in about 1940, it wasn't essential or relevant to the war. They didn't want bricks, they wanted bullets. It got closed down, so I went to Varleys from there. They used to make tank turrets, Churchill tank turret wheels and all sorts. I was there when they bombed it. When I was eighteen, I went in the army. When you were seventeen and eight months, you went to Renshaw Hall for your medical, so that you were ready to go in at eighteen straight away. But, just as I was about to go in, the war finished. I still had three nice years in the army which I enjoyed. They didn't really want a glut of engineers, so they put me in the medical corps, I enjoyed it. I was in Salonica for about eighteen months, and then we had a few months in Athens, and then we went to South Africa.

Roy Burrows

Loved Being on The Buses

I used to work on the buses as a 'clicker' – I was on there for a long while, and then I worked at Pilks. I used to love being on the buses, we used to have some fun. I was on the circle to Prescot and then I went on the Southport and then the Ravenhead – I went all around. We used to meet some very good people and also some very funny people. I remember some blokes getting on my bus on one day and they were fooling on, and they gave me this ticket, so I punched it – it was their dinner ticket! They couldn't get their dinners then because I'd punched their tickets.

Doris Hundley

The Rainhill Watchmaker

There was a fellow called little Joe and he was in Rainhill, the mental institution. They were sending them out for rehabilitation, so the managing director sent for me, and said that because I was over the union did I mind these people coming in, and I said that I didn't. About a dozen used to come along in a mini-bus, and I said that I would look after them even though they weren't in the union.

Now this chap was good, he'd been a watchmaker. If you gave him a watch then he'd just undo it, and within a few minutes he'd fixed it. But, that was on his good days. On his bad days, if you gave him a watch then he'd just put it into a vice, and it would be smashed up. So the people had to watch me. If I gave the thumbs up then it was OK to give

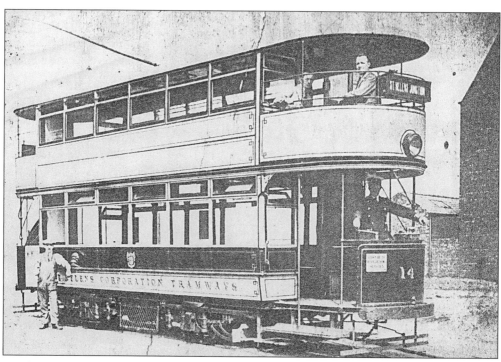

Work on tram electrification started in 1898 and electric trams were introduced into St Helens in 1899.

Members of the Sutton Camera Club on a visit to Bold power station, 1990.

him the watch, but the thumbs down meant to keep away from him. He became that good that they asked him if he wanted to work any overtime, so he said that he couldn't work Saturday's at time and a half because he had a girlfriend and they went shopping, but he could work Sunday's at double time. So, every Sunday he came in without fail, and he was on double time. Anyway, on this particular Sunday morning he didn't come in, so everyone was asking where little Joe was – they just couldn't understand it. Anyway, he came in about quarter to one and said that he'd had a puncture and had had to go back to the hospital to fix it, so he worked from one o'clock until five o'clock. The following week he told me that he hadn't been paid enough. I

looked at his card and told him that he was being paid at double time. He'd worked for four hours, so he'd been paid for eight. He insisted that he'd worked more than four hours. I told him that he'd worked from one o'clock to five o'clock which is four hours. He disagreed with this, stating that he'd worked one o'clock, two o'clock, three o'clock, four o'clock and five o'clock – a total of five hours! Just then the foreman came over, and asked me if there was any trouble. I told Joe to repeat what he'd said to me which he did. The foreman then put his fingers up and tried to explain using the spaces between his fingers. Joe asked the foreman which school he'd attended, and when being told that it was Preston Grammar School, Joe told him that at

Sutton Oak engine shed, which is now the site of Morrison's supermarket.

his school they counted fingers not spaces!

Tommy Dingsdale

Bad Luck Family

Mother, Helen-Ann her name was, was the eldest and had to find some work, so she used to work for Dr Dowling who practised just round the corner. Dr Dowling's wife was an Italian lady, very quick tempered, and mother didn't really like working for her very much. From there she went to work at what was Garswood Hall – I suppose at one time it was a house belonging to wealthy people, and there she met a young man, Jack Smith I think his name was, and he had come from Alderley Edge to do gardening. They fell in love, and they got married. They knew someone out in Canada who wrote to them and suggested that they should go out to Canada – so he went off to Canada, and eventually sent for mother and the two little girls to go and see him and stop with him in Canada. So, mother packed up – he sent her the tickets and everything, and two little fur coats for the little girls – and they were sailing on the Lusitania. They went to the docks, got on the boat, and then she decided that she wasn't going, so she came off the boat with the kids. Now, that boat sank! So, young Jack decided that if she wouldn't go over there, then he must go home. He came back to Saint Helens, and the only job that he could get was in the pit. He'd only been working in the pit for a week and there was the Wood Pit disaster and he got killed. If mother had have gone out, she would have been drowned with the girls – he came back and he got killed during the first week that he was at work.

Joan Gleave

A Bookie's Runner

My dad used to be a bookie's runner. He used to sort it all out in the parlour. You couldn't go near the parlour door, else you'd get your hands chopped off. There was a man called Johnny Lofthouse in Westfield Street, at the top end. It was all houses then, and he lived in one of them. My dad used to be his runner.

Josie Beard

Dad Put the Kibosh on That

I worked in a fruit shop but I didn't stay there very long and then I went to work in a grocer's shop. My mother was ill for a while, so my dad had me stay at home to look after her. I went into a shoe shop. I was still there when war broke out, and then after that I went into a factory. I was sixteen when war broke out. I went to Ravenhead first, but then I went to BI. At BI we were covering wire with cotton. All the work was for the forces. When they started to advance there was a lot of cable used. We covered the single wire, but then they were made up into huge cables, but in another part of the factory. I worked at Ravenhead first – I worked on glass there. They used to make fancy mirrors with glass, and there was coloured glass around it. We used to bevel the edges on a water wheel. After that I worked in shops, and I did that up to the time I was sixty-three. I much prefer working in shops than in factories. I should have been in the forces, but as my mother was ill, my dad got me exempt. I wrote about joining the RAF and I was due to be called up, but I couldn't go in the RAF unless my father or mother was in the services or my

Turbine machinery inside Bold power station.

boyfriend was either deceased or a prisoner of war. I couldn't get in under any of those categories! I was due to go into the army, but my dad didn't want me to go. I would have liked to have gone away and if I had got the choice I would have gone as stewardess on a liner, but my dad put the kibosh on that – I was still under twenty-one, and ships were being torpedoed, and he wouldn't let me go.

Beat Dingsdale

Worked as a Nurse Maid

When I left school I worked at the pottery making teapots. That was over the Kimick and the sand beds and it's called the Bates Pottery. My dad didn't like me working there because some of the men came out with bad language, so he made me stop. I went as a nursemaid at Varleys. I looked after their son, John, and I loved that. There was Mr George Varley and Mr William Varley. They used to run the iron foundry. We went on holiday for a month to Sile Croft in Cumberland. We had a caravan. There was a maid and a cook – they came with us. We had the caravan, and they had the big house. I was there to look after John, whilst Mr and Mrs Varley used to go off! They used to play tennis in the garden, they were beautiful big gardens in the house in Hurst Finch View. It was a beautiful place. It's not there now, it's just a field now. They had horses and everything there, but I was never one for riding the horses, I was never keen although I loved them. I left there to get married. I was married at twenty.

Margaret Winstanley

Foster's Glassworks

When I first left school I worked at Foster's Glassworks. My dad didn't like that because it had a name. My dad was old fashioned. When the war broke out we had to go on to war work, and I went to Prescot wire works, making ropes for the navy.

Josie Beard

When it Rained His Shoes Went Black!

We had no showers in the factory, so I had to get some put in. I got chatting to the bloke that was in charge of it. One day I went in and he was wearing a pair of lovely brown shoes, they were really polished. I asked him how he managed to get them so shiny. He insisted that they weren't new shoes and that he'd had them for about five years. I asked him what he used to polish them, as they looked brand new. He said that all he ever did was to put water on them, the only trouble was that when he put water in them they went black. He said that later on they went brown again. He also said that when he was out, he always knew when it was raining because his shoes went black!

Tommy Dingsdale

Sankey Canal close to St Helens town centre.

The old sheeting sheds near Reginald Road, Sutton, 1988.

Red Raddle on the Clogs

Seddon Street where I lived is near Pilkington's, and we always knew who worked at Pilkington's. When it rained there was red raddle on their clogs, and you could see all the footsteps with red raddle going straight to the front door. Red raddle was a mixture used for polishing glass. It's a very, very red substance, but if it got into the pores of your skin, then it took days and days to get out. You had to keep washing out all of the time. They even knew when certain people hadn't been to work – if it was raining and there was no red raddle leading to the door, then nobody had been out.

Ken Dale

Turning off the Lights

I met a guy who was complaining about having to go home at seven o'clock whereas another fellow in the factory was going home at half past seven. I had no idea why, but I said that I would find out. I went to the foreman and asked why one chap went home at seven and the other one didn't finish until half past. The foreman came back and told me that this fellow had been there for so many years, so, when everyone else had finished, he went around and switched everything off. I told the other fellow the reason. As I was telling him he turned his cap so the peak was on one side – I always knew when he was in a temper – I told him not to be

The No. 133 trolleybus, once a familiar sight on the streets of St Helens.

Trams and trolleybuses shared the streets for many years.

annoyed as it was not my fault. He then told me that he'd worked in the factory for over twenty years, and that he could go around in the dark and switch off all of the lights!! He was still telling this same story until the day that I left.

Tommy Dingsdale

Cabbage Hall Farm

I've actually spent nights in the shippens at Cabbage Hall Farm. If we had a couple of cows that were not too good, I was that wrapped up with this job, that I'd stay there. There was a passageway behind where all the cows were, and we used to throw the straw and the hay over, and that's where we used to sleep – it was lovely and warm. The other farm at Moss Bank is still there, but the Cabbage Hall Farm is now a housing estate.

Ken Dale

Vincent's Ice Cream Business

I got stuck into the ice cream business. I worked for a small local firm initially. Their trading name was 'Vincent's', my first name. I worked there for sixteen years in all. In the later years I went self-employed and I hired a van off them, and then I could trade, legitimately, using the name 'Vincent'. I was doing that until 1976. There were a few ups and downs, like vans not starting in the mornings, or getting punctures. By and large I enjoyed it. It was a fairly good life, and it was paying a lot better than Pilkington's were paying. But then you get to the stage when – I was thirty-five – you start thinking about whether you want to be doing this when you're fifty or fifty-five. The ice cream business is not just a summertime job like a lot of people think. First of all, in the temperature inside the van goes in excess of 100°F because it's all glass. In the winter it's absolutely freezing. You had to carry on through the winter, because if you didn't, then you'd have no customers when it came round to spring. People are creatures of habit, so you've got to keep going and be in the same place at the same time, so that they keep coming. We used to sell sweets and chocolates, and, for a spell, we actually sold cigarettes as well.

Vincent Woodward

An RAC Scout

My dad was with the Air Ministry police at Burtonwood. He used to say that aeroplanes were looking for Burtonwood, but they couldn't find it because it was in a hollow. He had long service with the Air Ministry police there. Before that he was an RAC scout on the East Lancs Road, and he used to ride along there on his push-bike. When they were building the bridge that leads to Pilkington's lodge there, the workmen were laughing at the men on one side of the road, because it was raining on one side of the road, but not on the other.

Edith Blackmore

Nursing at Rainhill

I worked in Rainhill Hospital. When I first left school I worked at Beechams. When I left school I was fourteen, and I went to

A laden goods train on the incline out of St Helens.

Beechams, and during summer I went working in the Isle of Man. There used to be a shop in town called Turners, it was a greengrocers and it also sold flowers. I used to work there, and one of the daughters, Totty Turner lived on the Isle of Man. Her name was Mrs Burrows, and her husband used to drive the buses on the island. They owned a hotel there – well, a guesthouse. After that I went working for Feeney's which was a bake-house. They had a bake-house at Union Street. One of the brothers was a milkman, and their mother used to live at the bottom of College Street. I worked at Sam Feeney's until after I was married. I then went to Rainhill Hospital and did my SEN there. I worked at Rainhill Hospital for about twenty-eight years, and I loved every minute. I used to nurse old

people. They were called EMI patients – elderly and mentally infirmed patients. I stayed there until 1991 when Rainhill Hospital shut down. I then went working at an old people's home at Toll Bar. I worked there for about eight months until I had to go into hospital with colitis and after that I had a stroke. I liked working with older people.

Iris Briscoe

Shave for Mr Birkhead

Our shop was a wholesale cigarette shop and we sold to other shops as well as having the sweets and the gent's hairdressing. When I got to about twelve my uncle, who was a lovely man, started not to be very well. The doctor used to say that it was his nerves, so I used to help uncle in the shop. People used to come in for a shave – we were near to the Town Hall, and all of the Town Hall bosses used to come in for a shave. I used to be the lather girl, so I used to lather ready for uncle to shave. Birkhead's shoe shop was up the road, and Bert Birkhead came in nearly every day for a shave. One day I said to him, 'Mr Birkhead, will you let me shave you?' He asked my uncle what he should do – my uncle was non-committal, saying that it was just up to him. I got the straight razor and stropped it. I was doing ever so well until I got to his Adam's Apple – it kept bobbling up and down, and I started to giggle and Uncle said that that was enough.

Joan Gleave

Counter Had Never Done so Well

I always seemed to drift from one job to another – I did it purposely. I went somewhere one day, and when it was over they came up to me and asked me if I wanted a job, I said that it would depend upon what the job was. It was a job at Woolworth's, so I landed there. I was on the garden counter, and I got settled in, and I fought like mad with the manager – we never agreed. We fell out like mad. One day I was in the understock fixing things and I heard a Mr Wilson, who was on the floor learning the job of managing talking about me. The manager's name was Newton. He said something to Mr Wilson, and Mr Wilson asked why I was

An aerial view of Bold power station, 1955.

Mrs Fenny, the coal woman with her horse and cart in Chester Lane.

never told off. Mr Newton said that he couldn't tell me off because the counter had never taken money like that before! I thought to myself that it was a weapon for me for the future. We still didn't stop fighting.

I can't remember how long I was with them, but it was quite a while. Every so often we got a rise in wages. I was doing very well, and Mr Newton came to me one day and asked who all the chaps around the counter were. I said that I didn't know, as far as I was concerned, they were only customers. He told me that they were all farmers from Prescot. I said that that's where all my information

was coming from. They used to discuss things with me, like what should be selling at a particular time. Time went on and I was still having rows. One of the girls came over to me one day from the electrical counter, and she told me that she'd just met Mr Newton. Just a few weeks later he died. I don't know what he died of, but everyone came and told me from all of the different counters. Very shortly after that I was offered another job, but it was more of a knockabout job. I didn't stick in one place. One person came and asked me if I'd go to Marks and Spencer's, but I didn't like the look of it. They were a bit uppity then, so I didn't

The view looking towards Rainford – there were two passenger lines and a freight line.

want to go. I can't remember what happened at different places, but I can remember that I had twenty-six years at the Providence. I went all though the different big shops in St Helens, just doing what I felt like doing, and then finishing and going on to something else. I landed in a nursing home, I can't think of the name of the place, it wasn't here in St Helens, I think that it was somewhere in Yorkshire. I've had a really good life, and, looking back on it now, I'm just sorry that I didn't put it down on paper because I would have enjoyed reading it back again.

Margaret Sill

The Miners' Strike in 1926

I remember the miners' strike. We lived at Thatto Heath, so all of the miners used to walk past our house on the way to work – there was King Pit, Queen Pit. They all had names, but the miners went on strike. It was in 1926. They used to come in the back entrance into Parliament Street. There were big open playing fields there, and all the people waited for the 'blacklegs' as they were called, to come through. The mounted police used to be there as well – they were trying to guard the 'blacklegs'. Everyone used to shout obscenities, even us kids, but we didn't know what we were shouting. My dad was a miner and he was on strike. We used to get food parcels sent to us from somewhere, and the Salvation Army did quite a bit. People who weren't in the mines and still working also helped out – everybody pulled together.

Tommy Dingsdale

I Was a Dilutee

My earliest memories were when I was eighteen, I was a senior, and I got called up. I was in the forces then until 1946, but, apart from all of that, I was started to work when I was fourteen. I went to school at Sacred Heart. We did a lot of rugby there and other sports – we didn't work very hard at other things! I enjoyed my time at school. I don't suppose that they enjoy it now, but I enjoyed it. I actually started work when I was nine, because there was not much money knocking about then. In fact, there was no money knocking about then – everybody was on the dole! I started work taking papers round for a few bob. When I left school, I went to the bottle works, UGB – that's closed down now. I worked there for twelve months, and work was beginning to pick up then, because in 1938 things were coming up! From there I went working outside on the buildings, and from there I was called up in 1941. I was in the Far East with the paratroops, in the Special Air Service. We were supply dropping. I was out for six weeks before I had to start work. I started to work for Pilkington's in 1946. I was a glasscutter in Pilkington's. The cutters were called journeymen, and they used to serve their time. With me, I was what they call a 'dilutee'. I then went to No. 6 warehouse as it was called, and I worked there from 1952 until the strike in 1970. From there I was transferred up to Cowley Hill, and then I was made redundant in 1981.

Harry Lynch

Iron in the Pinnies

I had my family after the war, I had two girls. My husband was in India for four years. I worked at Pilks during the war in the sewing room. I used to sew overalls and things like that. We used to put iron

Eugene Avenue – the scene of some poverty at this time, early 1950s.

85

There was a frequent bus service between St Helens and Widnes.

in some of the pinnies, that was for when they went in the tanks.

Doris Hundley

Glass for the Searchlights

When I came home I went back on my job at Pilkingtons. I was in the casting hall where we casted the glass out of pots. I was in that job after I left school, when I was sixteen. In those days we made all the glass for the searchlights, and X-ray glass. I left the casting hall when it shut down, and I went onto the float glass finish. I worked on all of the experiments for that – that's when they shifted the red raddle. I went all over the world with Pilkingtons. I went out to America twice, South Africa, Australia, Japan and Spain. I had to finish work then because my legs gave out on me!

I remember a bad accident at work.

They were doing a repair on the furnace, a hot repair. The crane used to go down to the work in hand, where they were doing the jobs, and then they'd come back up. I had a chap on my shift, I was foreman at the time, and he was told to go up on the crown of the furnace to check some thermocouples, and the crane came back and crushed him. They got him down, but he died on his way to hospital. That was one of my very low moments.

One of the happy moments for us as workers was when we got the first Queens Award at Pilkingtons for the float finish. A lot of us went up to the canteen where they had a spread and everything for the lads who had worked on it. We all got a Queens Award badge, and that must be one of my happiest times.

I finished work at fifty-four – I've been finished twenty-one years now. I've been all around the world

Bill Barrow

The Smelting Works

I left school when I was fourteen, and I went to work in the smelting works – it was dirty working there. There were piles of antimony dust, and you couldn't breath properly, but in other ways it was a good place to be. There were always plenty of other lads about your own age, so there was always something to do. We were all mates, but there was still the occasional fight. You don't seem to get too much fighting these days, but a good fight would clear the air.

Derek Gittins

British Sidac

I went to Parr Central School, and I left there and went working in the mines. I

This chimney was 'dropped' on Sunday 29 March 1992.

The Ditton Dodger en route to St Helens Central Station.

Surveying and measuring for Bold power station when it was being built in the 1950s.

worked in the mines from 1954 until 1957. I worked in Ravenhead colliery. When I finished there I went to British Sidac, and I was there for twenty-five years. I was making cellophane paper. It was a good process, the caustic and viscous that makes the paper, and the rest comes from the trees.

John Lee

A New Potato Peeler

I left school at fourteen. When I went to school, they didn't have scholarships that you had to sit, and I was the top of the class every term, but I didn't get the chance to go to secondary school, because it was always, you, you and you – all those who owned businesses or had plenty of money. We were a big family. I used to weigh sugar at the back of the shop. I used to get five shillings a week, which is only twenty-five pence in today's money. I used to work very hard when I was fourteen. Anyway, my mother once lost her potato peeler, and they were ten pence in the shop, and we used to get a penny in the shilling spend, so I got five pence the first week and then five pence the next week, and then I went and bought her a potato peeler for ten pence. Later I went to night school where I learned shorthand and typing.

Mary Knox

CHAPTER 5
Leisure

Ken and Jean Dale enjoying a quiet drink together, 1955.

Two Week's Holiday in Golborne

As regards holidays, well, my dad came from Parr. He came from down Parr Road, and we were living at Thatto Heath then, and all we usually got then was a day out at New Brighton. But, once a year, my dad used to walk me from Thatto Heath, down through Peasley Cross to Parr – 121 Parr Road. I went there for a week's holiday, and all the kids were jealous because I was having a

week's holiday and they were still in Thatto Heath, and it was only in Parr! I used to go for walks down Parr Road, across the farmland at the back there, and I could see down where the dog track was, it was marvellous.

And then there was another stroke of luck. One of my aunties had married a fellow from Golborne who worked in the pit, so then I used to have two week's holiday in Golborne. So when people talk

Christmas Fair at Nutgrove.

about going to Italy and Greece like they do now, then obviously Parr and Golborne were our Italy and Greece of the day. My dad used to put me on the train at St Helens Central – not where it is now, it's where Lincoln House is; that's where the station used to be, and then I'd go off into the blue beyond. I then had to wait at Golborne Station and either my Uncle Jack or my Aunty Maggie would come and pick me up and take me there. Then I had two weeks at Golborne.

Tommy Dingsdale

You Could Dance Every Night

You could go out somewhere every night for a dance – not like now, the only place they've got to go is to pubs. You could go out to the Co-Op on a Friday, then to the Plaza on a Saturday and then somewhere else on Sunday. The baths used to have a dance, and so did Holy Cross. You could go dancing every night. Lads used to ask you for a dance and then take you back to your seat. They asked if they could take you home. I don't envy them today. They think that they have a good time, but it wasn't like when we were young.

Roz Moore

Dangerous Water

The quarry in Hard Lane was always a draw because it was dangerous. Unfortunately, a lot of young fellows lost their lives in the water. We used to try to make a raft and get from A to B, but one or two lost their lives.

Ken Dale

Going to the 'Congs' Church

We always used to have to wear our Sunday best to go to Sunday School. It was the same with our best shoes. There was a little church in Gerrard's Bridge. Everybody used to go to the 'Congs' church. It was the friendliest little place that there could be. There used to be the Junior Fellowship. Going to these places kept us out of trouble. On Sunday afternoon we used to go the 'YM' in town, the penny pictures. Anybody that hadn't got a penny used to be helped over the wall.

Brenda Barrow

We'd Pay for the Cruet

My dad used to work at Fosters, the glass place, and he always used to save up for holidays. We used to go to Blackpool every year. But, we used to go into a boarding house, and all we paid for was the room and breakfast. My mum used to go out and buy all the food and the landlady cooked it all for you. We used to go out in the morning and she'd either get beef or steak or whatever we were having and Mrs Curran, the landlady, used to cook it for us. I had one of the bills, and on that bill there would be a charge for the cruet – we had to pay for our salt and pepper! She used to charge for the vegetables, but we bought the meat ourselves.

Bessie Roughley

Two Week's Holiday at Gran's

Coming back to holidays. I used to get on my bicycle and ride over to a place near to

The 1987 pensioners trip from the Sutton Arms.

More trophies for the choir.

Ainsdale. It was a place called Sherdley Hill, and I cycled over to my gran's. That was a journey from Seddon Street, right through Ormskirk, and then it's about halfway between Ainsdale and Ormskirk. It's out in the country and I used to love it. When gran used to see me coming she'd say, 'Here's Ken, I'm alright now for a week or two.' When I left school at fourteen I decided to have a week's holiday before starting work. Anyway, the one week went to six! She wrote a letter, because there were no 'phones then, saying that I'd be staying for another couple of weeks. That was my holiday. I enjoyed that just as much as any holiday today – it was great!

Ken Dale

Chester Races

We used to have coal fires, and my dad would say, 'That fire could do with some coal. Go and get a lump of coal as big as your head to put on the fire' My dad also run a pub down Parr, the Oddfellow's Arms. It's just near to the fire station, and even the customers used to join in when the piano player started. The customers all used to go to Chester Races. They'd bring in a tanner a week – which was plenty then – everybody used to go. My dad used to collect coppers, and, as they went off, he'd throw them against the wall, and all of the kids would rummage for it.

Roy Burrows

When everyday life in St Helens got too hectic, Joan could retreat to her caravan.

Never Miss A Rugby Match

Being the youngest in the family I was ruined. Everywhere the lads went, I went – I was a tomboy. I loved rugby. I never miss a rugby match. I still go now, but I don't go to away matches any longer. I go to all of the home matches – I never miss a home match, I'm a Saints supporter. I used to be a Recs supporter when it was red and black. I used to go with my brothers, up Moss Lane and all around.

Josie Beard

We Didn't Have Holidays

We didn't have any holidays, but I can remember odd days. Next door to us got a coach, and they put a little stool right at the back in the isle for me. My dad was out of work for about ten years as far as I can remember. He was out of work when my older sister got

Mary and Joan Booth playing ball against a wall.

Sutton ladies attending a Bible Class.

married. We didn't have a lot of money. My mum cleaned and washed for different people, but I lost her when I was fifteen, and then my dad died eight years later. I've more or less brought my younger sister up; we're very close now.

Jean Dale

When the Errands Were Done

We always went out with a bottle of water and a sandwich – it was called a 'buttie' then. Some weekends we used to go to Carr Mill, where the water used to come down the steps. We used to sit on the banks – you could spend all day and all night there, there'd be no problems like there are today. Your mother never needed to come looking for you. The only thing was, we couldn't go out on a Saturday until all the errands were done. Mum knew that she wouldn't see us again until much later – you never came home unless you had to do, because we were enjoying ourselves that much.

Ken Dale

Model Aircraft at Red Rocks

I always wanted a powered model aircraft, but I never got one. I used to make those elastic powered ones. I used to make them fly, but they always used to end up coming to grief. The favourite spot for that in those days was what they called the Red Rocks. There were always a lot of model enthusiasts up there. In the park, even today, they have the power boats – that's in Taylor Park. Red Rocks is just further over from Taylor Park. We ended up building a school over there – I think that it's called Carmel College now. Two fellows were killed when we were building that – but I wasn't surprised. I'd just left the day that it happened. I'd been working in the same area too.

Tom Gornall

Paddy's Blunder

In 1936/37 we moved down to Parr, and there were plenty of open spaces down there, and we used to go to a place called Sutton Moss, and it was a big place, about ten or twelve times bigger than a field. It was full of old workings and diggings out of peat. Consequently, it was filled up and grassed on every side, and it was a haven for birds – blackcaps, yellow hammers, partridge, coots even, water hens, pied wags, sky larks – any sort of wild birds that you could think of was round that area. I used to love it. I used to go many hours just watching, not to do any damage, but to see what was happening. It was a big struggle between you and the birds, to get you away from where they were. You used to have to get used to their ways, and you'd find out how they were working, and then you'd find where their nest was. It was a lovely hobby that. Sutton Moss and Parr Blunder. That was an old chemical working – it was hollows and rubble everywhere. But there

A YMCA Bowling outing at St Bethel Mission, late 1950s.

Playing on the maypole – Thatto Heath Park, c. 1931.

again, it was a good habitat for birds, rabbits, hares – everything. There's four football pitches on the Blunder now. There used to be a tip there, but it was taken away during the war. It was actually called Paddy's Blunder. Parr football field is part of it now, just near the back of the fire station.

Roy Burrows

Days in New Brighton

On holiday, we always used to go to New Brighton. Dad used to have a week's holiday – he worked at the sheet works. We used to go to New Brighton to play on the sand. We went by train to Liverpool, and then we got the bus down to the docks, and then we went over on the boat to New Brighton. We always used to look forward to that – it was only a day, that's all we got. That's all my dad could afford. It's still in my memory, we always used to go to New Brighton. Also, we went to Moreton – that's near to New Brighton and West Kirby. We used to go cockling there – it was great. Even when we were coming home on the train, the cockles were still moving about in the bags! It was really lovely.

Margaret Winstanley

Fell under the Ice

Where the cows used to come and drink, it used to freeze over solid. We would go skating on it, but sometimes, just around the edges it hadn't frozen, so it meant that you had to jump over. On this particular day I jumped over, but what I hadn't seen was that there was a big hole in the ice – I jumped straight into the hole! I couldn't swim, and to this day, I can't tell you how I got out of that hole again. If I put my hand up to the ice then I slipped down – it was just a miracle. I kept bobbing up, and my head was hitting the ice, I can't remember anything more about it.

Ken Dale

Stonies and Other Games

We had a big black range, and my mother used to pile it full of toast in the morning, and then shout the five of us downstairs. We used to fight for the one at the bottom, because it was always very crispy. We used to have a season for everything like top and whip, tin can bung off – if you know what that is. Where the houses were, there was a space and there was a grid. We put a tin can on there, and the boys and girls – say about seven, eight, nine or ten of age, and the one that was on the bung as they called it, would have to run for it when it was thrown away, and all of the others would have to hide. When they all hid, the one that was on the bung had to go and look for them. But, if somebody could get to the grid and the tin can, they used to bang it. Another game was 'stonies', or marbles as it was sometimes called. In those days we didn't have flagged streets, they were all dirt and soil. We used to make a big ring and put the 'stonies' in, and then try to knock them out of the ring. My sister used to buy them, they were only five for a penny. She used to come out with these big gloves on, and she'd win them all back off them. People used to go and knock at my mother's door and say that our Joan was cheating.

Every June we had what they called a fair up the back entry. People had buckets of tennis balls or small ping-pong balls, or holes drilled in the ground and cigarette cards. So, it was one to play, and if you won – you got the balls in the buckets or down the holes or whatever, then you got two cards back. It was like using cigarette cards

Ready for the concert.

as money. These two ladies used to stand on the back gate with a table in front of them selling nettle pop which they used to make out of the nettles.

Mary Knox

Saving Seats at Dances

There used to be dances every Saturday in Reeve Hall, and we went there every Saturday. You used to have to go early to get your place, or you couldn't get in. We used to save the same seats at the same tables every time we went, and we had to go at seven o'clock so that we could get the same places. We used to save chairs for friends – otherwise other people would be sat there! It's funny because they had a club at Rainhill as well, and when we used to go to that club there were regulars who used to go and sit in the same places. One night I remember we went there and sat in this place and we could hear this person calling us – she was a sister at Rainhill Hospital. She was sat at the back of us, and it was only after that we found out that we were sitting in her seat. She used to sit next to the one-armed bandit, and put money into the bandit all night! She lived in the nurse's home. If anybody ever sat in my place then I'd be looking at them and calling them blind!

Iris Briscoe

We Made Our Own Games

I loved playing hopscotch and skipping rope when I was a girl. Also, we used to fly kites, but I was a tomboy. Well, you couldn't expect anything else having four brothers! We used to play hopscotch with a stone or chalk on the flags. Before the houses were built in Boundary Road we used to get clay off there and make cakes and then play cake shops. We'd make fancy cakes and decorate them with bits of grass and other things. I don't think that kids make as much fun today – they don't know how to play. I had a doll, which I've still got, but it's seventy years old now. We played with dolls and things like that. We used to trip around in a pair of someone's high-heeled shoes when we were kids. We used to dress up – the shoes where huge, but the high heels make you feel as though you were somebody, and when you carried your handbag. It was great.

Beat Dingsdale

We Used to Have the Lads In

Mum and dad were both jolly. They used to go to a place called Cheshworth's pub, it was at the top of Peel Street. My dad used to have to go in about seven o'clock at night, save my mum a place, and then she'd go along about nine o'clock. Dad used to go early to save her a place, so that she'd have a chair to sit in when she got there. While they were out, we used to have all the lads in. Where my mum lived in Peel Street, it was an end house and then there were two fields. On the opposite side near to Cooper Street is Cheshworth's. So, there used to be a gang of lads in, but when we heard my mum knocking at the front door, all these lads would rush out the back door. In those days we had yards, and at the bottom of the yard was the outside toilet, and, as soon as we heard the knocking at the door, all of these lads had to fly out of the back, so

LMS Rose Queen, 1930.

Members of the Sutton Historic Society setting off on their very first coach trip in 1987.

Tarantella in Rainford village hall, May, 1965.

they'd be running down the yard when my mum came in.

Iris Briscoe

Top Flower Show Prize

I turned out to be a florist. I went right to the top as a florist – I entered the Southport Flower Show at which I won the top prize. I was always interested in flowers and so it was a natural progression to go into shows, but when I got married all of that came to an end.

Mary Green

Field Days Were Great

I used to go to the Bible class at Balmer Street Mission, I was about eighteen or nineteen at the time. The wife, who's three years younger than me, she was pretty strong with the Church of England, but I talked her into coming along to the Bible class. We also used to have 'field days'. There was a procession of all the lads and girls, and there were toddlers as well – the girls were in their summer frocks and we were in our short pants. We'd walk down to a field in Thatto Heath where we used to have sports, and that was great. A 'field day' in our lives was a great event. It mightn't sound very exciting now, but it really was good at the time.

Tommy Dingsdale

Sherbet and a Bottle of Water

Bill used to go playing cricket and football with Pilkington's, everywhere was fields. The girls used to go and watch them and then the jazz bands used to come onto the fields. From our house, just over the fields, we could see right over to Eccleston, there was no more houses or anything, only farms.

We couldn't even afford the trams, so we had to walk a lot of the time. We used to go from my grandmas over the 'Mark' fields – it's now Merton Bank Road. We used to go over there and that was all Kimicks. We used take a bottle of water and some sherbet to put in the water, and we used to go as far as Carr Mill to where the water used to come down, I think that it was called the Seven Arches, or something like that. There was no East Lancs Road then.

Bessie Roughley

We Played 'Ledges'

We played what they called 'ledges'. All schools had low ledges, and we just used to draw lines, and you'd start off at the nearest

Relaxing here after an evening's concert are members of Haydock Male Voice Choir with their wives and girlfriends.

Harold Wilson is guest of honour at a Help the Aged Concert being held at Peasley Cross Labour Club.

line and bounce the ball, and then catch it. If you managed that then you went to the second line and so on.

Roz Moore

Playing Top And Whip

In the week we used to play top and whip. The top was a 'carrot top', which was solid and couldn't be knocked that much. We used to draw little circles on top or stick on a piece of silver paper, so it looked good when it was whizzing around. The mushroom-shaped ones were the best. If you hit them right, they used to spin in the air. It was good to run home from school and get out the whip and top. There was nothing on the roads in those days. All I can remember on the roads was the steam engines, and they used to run to the brickworks which was Roughsedges at Sutton Heath. There was a fire underneath, and the cinders used to drop onto the floor, so we used to have to watch where our tops were.

Tommy Dingsdale

We Always Copped Off

We used to go in a caravan now and again, but our real treat was going over to New Brighton on the boat. It was only a penny, and you'd get your ticket out of the slot machine, and then you'd carry on and go. That was great. The boat was called the Mona Castle I think, and sometimes we'd go on that. We really used to enjoy it – you could even get chips on board! We'd buy our chips, and then when we got to New

Showing off their trophies. Girls and teachers from the Carter School of Dancing.

Brighton, we'd get off and head for the sand, and that was it. And then as we got older, we still went, me and my mates, and there used to be soldiers there then. We always 'copped off' – that's what we went for! I was in the Women's Junior Air Corps and I had three stripes. What I got them for I don't know. The only thing that I can think of now is that I was good at gym.

Josie Beard

Nobody Goes Skating Now

We used to go on the old golf links near to Toll Bar where the proper golf course is now, Grange Park Golf Course. All the ground behind there used to be the old golf links, so in the winter, when it was snowing and there was ice on the ground, we used to make a sledge from wood. We also used to go over to Eccleston Mere, and we used to go skating on there. There were cold winters and warm summers. Nobody goes skating now because it never freezes over.

Tommy Dingsdale

Field Days from St Austin's

We used to go on field days from St Austin's. All the different classes in the school had various competitions – running, boxing and rugby. The field days were held on Scott's field at the back of the school. Somebody would always hit the ball over the railway cut. It was good playing there.

Derek Gittins

A few days away from St Helens. The annual holiday in Anglesey.

Walking to Billinge

In the summer when it was warm we walked as far as Billinge. It's about five or six miles away, but we walked there pretty often. My great-grandad used to live there, and my dad used to take me, and my old grandad used to tell me stories about Billinge. The story they used to tell me was that they had six white stonies and one coloured one. On a Monday they would take a white stoney out, then the same on Tuesday, Wednesday and so on, until Sunday when the blue stoney was taken out of the window – and then they went to church! We used to make the Billinge Calendar later when I taught engineering.

Tommy Dingsdale

A German choir enjoying the hospitality of Haydock Male Voice Choir.

Members of the Derby and Joan Club ready to set off for Paignton, 1968.

Dad's Holidays

My dad used to have one weekend off, and that was what he called his holiday. He used to walk us all down to Carr Mill Dam, and we used to get a jug of tea and carry sandwiches down. There used to be water coming down the steps at Carr Mill, and we used to paddle there – that was our holidays. By the time we got home after having walked there and back, we were that tired that we were glad to have a wash and then go to bed.

We used to have one bath that used to come out in front of the rug. My mother always put soda in the water, but they tell you not to use soda now – but all of us have good skin, so it didn't do any of us any harm. The eldest one used to wash everyone's hair, and there were six of us with long hair.

Brenda Barrow

Post a Letter on the Last Tram

They used to run the trams down Nugrove, round to Toll Bar and then back into St Helens. You could even post a letter on the last tram at ten o'clock at night! As you went past, there was the Empire cinema, but now it's the Empire Garage. Everybody went to the pictures then. When I first went they were all silent pictures. The words used to come up at the bottom of the screen, and a lot of people used to read the words aloud for people who couldn't read. Looking back now, many people couldn't read or write. It was a bit annoying really, because as you were trying to concentrate on the picture, other people were reading out aloud. In front of the screen there was a violinist and a pianist, and sometimes we were more distracted by watching them than watching

Ken Dale relaxing in his garden at Billinge, 1960.

the film. After the cinema we'd go across to the park, and then we'd either be cowboys and Indians or Tarzan. We used to climb up the trees when we were pretending to be Tarzan.

Tommy Dingsdale

Sandwiches, Pop and Crisps

On the last Saturday of the summer holidays we used to get together and have a May Queen procession. Our parents used to make the dresses with crinkle paper, and we used to walk around a few streets in the area with a little collecting box, and my sister used to play the kazoo, and another one of my friends used to ring a bell. When we'd finished our collection we went to the little corner shop and bought paste and we made sandwiches, and we had pop and crisps. We all went to my Aunty Polly's and we had a tea party, and then we played games. It was really good – we had a brilliant time.

Mary Knox

Played in Parr Public Band

My grandad used to be brass band mad, and he passed it on to me – I love bands. He was in Nutgrove Band which was a prize band in those days. It's gone out of existence now. My grandad started to teach me when I got to thirteen or fourteen. I used to play in Parr Public Band. I've done about thirty-seven contests, but I didn't think that I could do any of them because I used to get frightened going up on the stage! Old Tom started the band years ago. I can't remember his other name, but he was always known as Old Tom. If you played a wrong note and he had to tell you more than once, then you got a belt around the ear hole! We used to go carolling with the band – I really enjoyed it. I had one of those little 'noddy' cars then, one of those three-wheelers. I used to carry all of the music for the band in my car. At that time I was still playing myself. I used to play cornet to start with, then tenor horn – I loved the tenor horn. I then went on to play the flugelhorn, which is next to a tenor horn – in between a tenor horn and a cornet. I did try once to play a double bass, but I couldn't. It was too big and I was only a 'dot' – I was only small. We used to play at St 'Vint's' School field days

Derek Gittins

A young Mary Knox (5 years) enjoying dressing up with some of her friends.

Nutgrove Methodist Men's Choir.

Biked it Everywhere

I raced pigeons from 1948, and I biked it all the way to Whitchurch let them go, and they came home and I was only halfway back! In 1976 my mother was in Clatterbridge Hospital, and I biked it there too – two days running, Saturday and Sunday – 180 miles. I went over the Runcorn Bridge and then out towards Frodsham.

John Lee

Little Black Velvet Pants

I was in a dancing troop and I was the comedian. It was Joe Saxon's Troop – he worked at Pilkingtons. He was a big boss at Pilks, and he had this dancing class. We used to go all over everywhere – Blackpool, London and the Isle of Man. There was dancing, singing and club swinging – all that sort of stuff. It was great in them days. We used to wear little black velvet pants and white satin blouses with a black bow. When I was in the Saxon Troop we used to go to the Stanley Park in Blackpool, and there used to be a big festival on every summer, and we used to entertain. It wasn't just us, there were lots of other people there too. And then we used to go to the Isle of Man every year for the ballroom dancing, and my daughters used to come along. I used to go with them to be a dresser. They used to have their numbers on their backs.

When I was the comedian with the troop, we used to have a school scene and I was Jacky Jones with a cap on. I always used to give the wrong answer, and the

Senior Citizens' party at the Rifle, 1968.

A proud Bert Gleave with the prize-winning Haydock Male Voice Choir.

teacher always used to get me out, and she had a stick with a clapper on the end. I used to have to bend down and she'd whack me. When I was pregnant I was still in the troop, and Joe Saxon used to say, 'Don't hit her, she's having a baby.' He used to be in the wings, and he'd ask them not to hit me hard. It's little things like that that are amusing now – but it wasn't at the time!

Josie Beard

The Bungalow Bath

Someone told me that they had a 'bungalow' bath, and I thought that they were ever so posh because they had this 'bungalow' bath. But when it all came to,

it was just the same one as what we had – a tin one hanging up in the back yard. That used to come out once a week, every Saturday night, and we were all put in, one after the other. Then there were the washing days with the rubbing board and the boiler, and the 'dolly blue'. When I started to grow up, we started to go to dances, but there aren't very many now. We had somewhere to go every night – the Oddfellow's Hall, Holy Cross, Co-op, the baths. We used to have some fun on the fairground, and if we went to the pictures, somebody would save a place for us. By the time that we were finished then there'd be about ten of us. That was another thing, we used to go to one where they only had forms and there were lanterns. You'd sit on the form, and if you were at the end, then,

Putting on a show. This is a production of Slow Boat to China *at Rainford Village Hall, May 1965.*

Annie Douglas on holiday.

before you finished you'd be on the floor, because people would be pushing up all of the time.

Mary Knox

Len Johnston's Boxing School

I remember, just before the war, they used to have the visiting Silcock's fairs, and there was always a good boxing booth on, it was called Len Johnston's. His brother was one of the fighters. I can see him now announcing – this is Len Johnston's Boxing School. Introducing Billy, brother to myself – that was Billy Johnston – they

were both darkies. Then there was Jack Lydon from Birkenhead, Dixie Kidd from South Wales. But Jack Lydon – it was said that he had killed a man – and he was telling the truth probably! He used to go through all of the names, but those few still stand out in my mind. You had to beat them to get your five bob, or whatever! They were good days.

Roy Burrows

The Veterans Club

We both used to go to the YMCA, but I was always on the committee, because I was always the driving one. I used to organise holidays for them and days out. On a Wednesday, we used to have a little church meeting there, upstairs, and then we used to play dominoes. They had this committee, it was called the Veterans Club then, and then it was changed to the Pensioners Club. We used to go to Pitlochry – the place there belonged to the YMCA. We also used to go to Lowestoft. I also used to organise days out. I did this for quite a few years, and then I gave up when my husband was ill.

Hannah Kelly

CHAPTER 6
Other Times

Charles and Elizabeth Critchley immediately before their wedding in 1925.

I Went in as a Pilot

When the war started I wanted to go into the RAF flying, because, before the war, I wasn't good enough to be educated up to the standard to navigate or pilot. So, when the war started, they said that if you were good enough, and daft enough, to go up there then it didn't matter so much, as long as you

could pass all of the exams. First of all I went in as a pilot, but I had a few problems. You had to go on test runs with a test pilot, and this fellow that we had, everybody disliked him – he was a terrible bloke. He didn't want to do this kind of thing in the war, he didn't want to be in training, and if he could do anything that would make it awkward for you, then he did it! We used to fly in a Tiger

Moth, they were biplanes. You had to keep your eye on the ring which held the struts together, because that was the way to keep straight and level, by keeping this little ring on the horizon. He sat at the front and you sat at the back being the trainee, but you were doing the flying. You had to keep your eye on this ring to keep flying horizontal. In order to see the ring we had cushions tucked underneath our parachutes. On one day when I went there were no cushions there, so I went dashing back to the billet, got a blanket and put that underneath. What I didn't know was that, instead of just taking off and landing and doing all this kinds of things, this fellow decided that he would do loops, spins and then come out of them, which is OK, except that when we were

Sitting on The Ledge in St Helens, 1957.

doing one of the spins, the blanket slipped out. It went onto my knees and I couldn't put the stick back, so we were gradually going down and down, and I couldn't get it back again. I could see by the ring that we weren't level on the horizon. He said to me, 'Put your hands up in the air.' That was to see if I had hold of the stick. He asked me if my legs were catching the stick. I told him that it was the blanket. He then asked me if I was cold! I couldn't tell him why I had the blanket there. He said that he would 'put it on it's nose', and I could then snatch it out. I pulled the blanket out, and when we landed he went to the far end of the airfield which was about two miles away. He threw the blanket out and then told me to jump out and get it. As soon as I did he roared off back again, and left me to walk all the way back. When I got there, there was a hell of a stink. He said that I could have killed him, I could have destroyed the aircraft – nothing was said about me! I had to go before a board in Manchester, and, because I had very good navigation marks, they decided to give me a navigation test. I was lucky in that respect because, when I got married, my best man was a navigator in the navy, so, although it's a different kind of navigation, at least he put me onto the right track, so I knew all the basics. I had 97 exams and I failed 4. I had to re-sit them, passing them, and that proved that I had ability, but I couldn't achieve that at school because we were poor. That gave me a lot of satisfaction.

Tommy Dingsdale

'It Was A Bit Rocky Last Night!'

And then there were the war years when the bombings used to happen. My mum used to

Fenny's Lane in 1920.

load the old pram up with blankets and eiderdowns, and she'd take me and my younger sister, every night automatically round about four o'clock, all the way up North Road down again to the 'Congs' church which is now the NatWest bank. We used to go down in the bowels of the church. I never understood why my father didn't come down with us. I found out later that his view was that if he was going to go, then he was going to go in bed! He never missed going to bed all through the war. He was a moulder, and they wouldn't have him in the army because he was making propellers at Liverpool for the ships. He never got up and went under the stairs or nothing. Often when my mother got home he would make a comment such as, 'By God Lizzie, it was a bit rocky last night!' When we were in the bowels, we only heard the odd thump. You can never forget those things.

Ken Dale

Grandma Brought Me up in Parr

I was born in 1917 and by the time that I was eighteen months old my mother had died in the war, the First World War. She died in the flu epidemic, so my grandma brought me up in Parr. My dad got married again when I was three, and fortunately the family that he married into just accepted me. I could have been ignored, but I wasn't. I used to go to my grandma's every weekend.

They allowed me to go there then and every holiday. Sometimes stepmothers used to stop you going to your relations. I had a good childhood. We were poor as were a lot of people. When I was at my grandmas I used to sit on the doorstep, they lived in Ashcroft Street in Parr. I used to sit there and watch the 'collars' go to work – I meant the colliers. They were going to Sutton or somewhere.

Bessie Roughley

To Meols in a Pinny

We lived with my grandmother until we went down Oxford Street. She used to

We have loved him in life, let us not cease until we have introduced him by our tears and prayer into the house of the Lord—St. *Ambrose*.

✝

OF YOUR CHARITY PRAY FOR
THE SOUL OF

Alfred Ernest Jackson,

WHO DIED OCTOBER 23rd, 1906,

AGED 10 YEARS,

And was interred at Sutton Monastery
October 28th.

——o——

You must not cry my mother dear,
And wish me back again ;
But think how sweet 'twill be for me,
To suffer no more pain.

Isaac Ashton, Undertaker, Sutton.

A memorial notice from 1906.

make pop in a big stone jug. She made dandelion, and they used to come from miles around for the pop. We used to stir the pop and then bottle it. Sometimes she made sarsaparilla. At Christmas my grandmother used to be skinning rabbits for everybody. She had us all plucking chickens, but I couldn't do it now. She used to get a lit paper and singe all the feathers off. There was a family across the road from us, we lived in Morley Street then, it was a big family and there was only one girl. Not one of them was ever in trouble and they all turned out to be very clever and they all got very good jobs. They lived in a two-bedroomed house like us. Sometimes they used to go to Meols camping. She used to have a pinny on and she would be pushing an old trolley, and they'd be going off to Meols, and they'd stay there for a few weeks in a tent.

Brenda Barrow

The 'Liverpool Woman'

My mother used to refer to the 'Liverpool woman'. It was a lady who lived just a few streets away – but we all knew exactly who she meant. If she said that today in St Helens it wouldn't be helpful at all, because many people have moved in from Liverpool, to the advance of St Helens I might add. I think that with housing only being available outside of Liverpool, all Liverpool having been built up, I think that a lot of the go-ahead people from Liverpool finished up in St Helens, and I certainly mean for the better. I'm not a St Helens person who says, 'Send them all back', quite the reverse! I think, even on a political front, some of the political leaders that we've had in St Helens from Liverpool, would have made Liverpool a lot better – had they have applied their talents.

Brian Coxhead

Monday Was Washday

Monday was always washing day, inevitably. We always knew what was going to happen on Monday, and then on Tuesday – if everything was dry – it was ironing. The iron was an old-fashioned iron. There was no heating in it, so you had to put it in front of the fire, and it was the heat from the fire that warmed it up. Mother used to spit on it to check if it was warm enough. On Wednesday it was usually tidying up, going around to see if the house was in order. Thursday it was dusting and more messing about like that. Friday was pay day, so she had to go down and buy the food in for the weekend. She used to go down on late Saturday nights, there were no fridges then, so they had to sell or give everything away. You could buy a rabbit, potatoes, carrots and turnips – you could get all of those for one shilling. On Sunday we went to church, and there was nothing else. Mother cooked the meal, and then that was it on a Sunday. And then the week started all over again.

Douglas Ashton

Given Beer at Work

My father used to be a drinker. We used to get thrown out every Saturday night, but he didn't hurt anybody, it was just that he drank so much, but they all did then. They used to give them beer at work, he was a bottle hand. He worked at UGB. I don't know why they gave them beer, but that's what got him off.

Doris Hundley

All The Way From Prescot

Well, it was during the war when it was blackout, and the buses had stopped running, so you walked home, and I've walked on my own all the way from Prescot and I wasn't a bit afraid, but I wouldn't walk out today! We lived in Penrith Road at Portico on the Portico estate. I worked at the BI at Prescot that's where they held the dances.

Beat Dingsdale

Games in Clinkham Wood

When I moved to Clinkham Wood we spent all of our time in the woods, just climbing trees and finding secret places. Somebody once left some old tractor wheels, and we spent hours just swinging on them. We found so much to do as young children – it was incredible. And that wood now, well – it's been made into a conservation area. I read an article in the paper, saying that people were complaining because there was nowhere for the children to go, because the woods is now out of bounds. I couldn't believe it because I had such a happy childhood – we didn't have much money.

Roz Moore

Tommy Maloney and Eric Coffey sharing a few drinks at the Beehive, Moss Nook.

A Smoking Lesson

There were two sisters older than me, and two brothers younger than me. Since those days, our feelings for each other have always been the same, and I put it down to the strict upbringing that we had, because my father he was very, very, and I mean very, strict. At the same time, if there was sickness he was a good male nurse. I used to come home on leave from the army, and I could see a change in him over the years, until such time, when I got demobbed, he'd have the cleaner on, he'd be polishing, he'd be putting the washing out and what have you. It was a complete change – I suppose that was old age! I always looked up to him – he was a fine bloke.

He was strict. I remember the time when there was about five or six of us knocking about together. In those days, in Kirkland Street, there used to be a slot machine outside of the newsagents, and you could buy three cigarettes and three matches for a penny, and we got these and then went in this back entry, smoking away. Eventually, I could feel myself feeling sick, so the first thing that I did was to dash home, and we lived in a two-up, two-down. I dashed through, my mother was baking in the back kitchen, and I'm trying to get to the toilet at the bottom of the yard. I couldn't make it – I just made it into the yard over the drain, and I was being sick there. I heard my mother call for my father, and he came out. 'You've been bloody-well smoking' – thump! 'No I've not dad.' 'You've been bloody-well smoking' – thump! 'I'll cure you.' He went in and brought me a Woodbine out, and said that it would stop me smoking – I wish it had have done!

Henry Atherton

Dancing with a Broken Toe

I don't remember much about the war, only that I had a spell working at the bake-house, but that wasn't classed as munitions, so I went working at the BI. I only worked there for about six months. It was when I was about sixteen, and we used to have big coils of wire, and I remember dropping one of these big coils of wire on my toe, and it broke my toe, but when you're young you do all kinds of things. I still put on my shoes to go dancing – I broke all of the plaster of Paris. It ended up just like a limp bandage, because I broke it all pushing my shoe on. I used to play on it for as long as I could. I remember the ration books which we were all given. We used to go and queue up for cakes. There used to be a shop in Duke Street, a bakery shop, and we used to go and get these rolls with cream in the middle. You had to queue up from seven o'clock in the morning because there'd be a big long queue at this baker's shop, because when they sold out that was it! You didn't get any, so we used to go early to get at the front of the queue to get the cakes. Chesterfield Bakery it was called.

Iris Briscoe

From Five Shillings A Week

There were five children in our family – we had six, but one died. My mother worked in a rug factory. She also took washing in for people and cleaned houses. Father worked three days a week. My brother, he's dead now, he won a scholarship. My sister is a retired deputy head, she won a scholarship. My other brother won a scholarship to Cowley and then to Manchester University – he became a PhD. I went to school until I was sixteen. From being fourteen, I got five shillings a week. I stayed on for that five shillings, because it paid for my mother and father to keep me there. First of all, I got a

Albert Perry's homecoming in 1947 at Penlake Pavilion.

The LMSR masked jazz band from St Helens Junction Station.

job in a wireless and cycle shop. I did the weekly payments for people for Christmas. Sometimes we worked till nine or ten at night. People saved up for something for Christmas – little bikes for the children, dolls and things. Later on I became a secretary and my other sister became a bookkeeper. We both worked until we were over seventy years old.

Agnes Bacon

Keep Pedalling!

We were devils in our days. We lived at the top of North Road where the Park Hotel and St Marks church are and I said to my mate Harry, one day, that I was jiggered. We still had to go all the way down City Road to our house at the bottom. We saw a bike propped up on the curb – they did it with the pedals then. I had a flash of inspiration. We decided that Harry would pedal, and that I would go down on the crossbar. We decided to go down the road, get off at the bottom, and then leave it propped up there. Unbeknown to me and Harry, we got onto the bike and set off, and we heard this shout. And, of all the bikes that we could have picked, it was the bobby's bike who just happened to be in the pub! He was shouting after us, but I just said to Harry to keep pedalling! He knew who we were, so he came to our house later that night. I protested that I had no intention of pinching the bike, and that it was just to get to the bottom of the hill – but it was his voice calling after us that I can still remember.

Ken Dale

Satisfied With The Money

On the first redundancy, before you got all this lot of money, they asked him if he would be redundant. He said no, because we'd just gone into our house at sixty. We moved in, and then they asked him again. He knew one or two men, he was on the staff you see, who had finished and they were quite satisfied with the money that they got. So, when they asked him again, he said that he would go if the money was alright. That was it, he never looked back.

Hannah Kelly

Couldn't Get Your Breath!

We had a tin bath and every Saturday night it was brought in front of the fire and we had a bath there, but we'd go into the back kitchen to wash our hair over the sink. Mother put a big black pan on the stove and she'd fill it again, and she'd pour that over your head for rinsing – you couldn't get your breath! As you grew a bit older, you went down to the swimming baths where they had private baths and you went for a bath down there. With them being so near, we all went down to the baths. I couldn't swim, but I used to try. I was pushed off the little steps leading into the water and that frightened

me, I was gasping. I didn't go for ages and ages after that even with the school. I used to make excuses and say that I'd forgotten my towel. But then, I thought to myself that I had to go, so I did it on my own. I went and just tried swimming a little bit until I got going. I then went with the school and finished it off then.

Jean Dale

Ran on the Bowling Green

Thatto Heath Park was fairly close by, and I had an uncle who worked at Parks and Gardens in those days – he was a very keen gardener, obviously. He looked after the

Off to their wedding – Thomas and Iris Briscoe, Boxing Day, 1949.

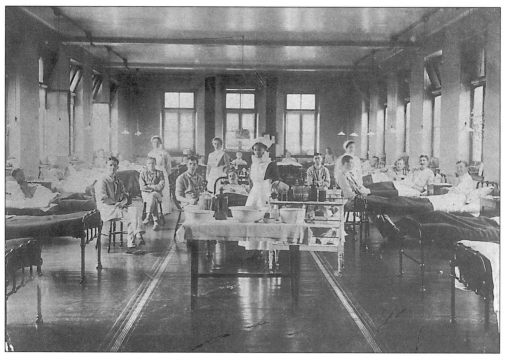

Casualties from the First World War recovering in hospital.

bowling greens, and he was a mad-keen cricket fan, and I've always been very interested in cricket myself. I remember once, another 'friend' of mine, dared me to run onto the bowling green, which of course, was totally unheard of – you just didn't do that sort of thing. So, for this 'dare' I ran onto the bowling green, and my uncle, who was about five hundred yards away on the other side of the park, saw me – I never lived it down!

Vincent Woodward

'I'm Not Having You'

It was just like when I had to get married – all hell was let loose in our house! My sister, the eldest, because I was the youngest of

them all, she lived higher up. My mum said, 'Go to our Lizzy, she'll take you, I'm not having you.' Everything calmed down after the initial shock – well, it does doesn't it? We've made a good marriage, and we've got a good family.

Josie Beard

Sat on a Settee under the Stairs

We had refugees coming from Liverpool to the mission, but we never met them. After the war it was known as Shelter Park, next to Thatto Heath Park. They had all underground shelters there. When the sirens went you had to go to these shelters. My grandfather was in his seventies, he was more of a father to me than my own father was. In fact, my father eventually left my mother and me in 1950. Anyway, we used to go rushing down to these underground shelters – they were smelly and not very nice places. My grandfather said that he'd had enough of this. So, we put the settee under the stairs, and when the sirens went we used to sit under the stairs on this settee – what good that would have done if any bombs had dropped I don't know! But there again, if there'd have been a direct hit on one of the underground shelters, then I don't suppose that they'd have had any chance anyway. With the terraced streets there was no such thing as Anderson Shelters, they were just for the well-to-do council house tenants in those days. I live in one of them now – when I was a kid that would be called middle class. We used to have to get bathed in front of the fire, in front of the Yorkshire range. We used to make a truck and go to the coal tip so that we could get coal for the fire, and it wasn't a choice – you either did that or you'd no fire!

Tom Gornall

Not Even a Water Closet

Every Saturday night there was always a fight around there when the men had been to the pub. It was a different life from what it is now. At night time they used to come and empty the toilets. They used to come with a big lorry, and they had big buckets. They used to go into the entries and, where the toilets were there were no water closets or anything like that. They used to have a little opening that they could just put these buckets in. You used to have to use these for your toilets and every week they used to come and take the old one and put a new

clean one in – it was awful! Where my grandma lived it was a communal yard, and there were five or six families used to use that yard, and they all had their own toilets. I used to hate going there. When my dad got married again we went to live in New Town and we had a proper toilet there, a water toilet!

Bessie Roughley

Little Nutgrove School Shelters

When the air raids started during the war, well, we used to go down to the shelters under Little Nutgrove School, and there they used to have people getting up and giving a song. They did anything to take our minds off the raids. I didn't care, I loved it. Little Nutgrove School was a gathering

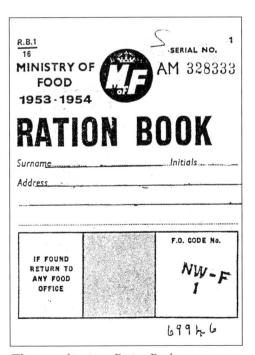

The once ubiquitous Ration Book.

point for all the people. The planes used to come over about seven o'clock as it was going dusk, and we used to all make for the shelters. It was like a cavern in there, and everyone had their own little corner – it was fantastic. Families used to talk down there that never spoke to one another from one year's end to the next! I was ten or eleven at the time. What I really loved about it was that my mother used to be there. We'd go to my gran's who lived in Nutgrove Road, and that's where we went from. We'd get there early to save our place. Afterwards we used to go around picking up shrapnel from the guns.

Derek Gittins

A studio shot of Mary and Joan Booth enjoying a 'day out' with Aunty Johanna and Uncle Bob.

Nine Guineas for Coffin and Best Shroud

My mother furnished a house for thirteen pounds. The bills are all dated 1908. There was a table and chairs, a big fender, a tidy, the beds, mats, two pictures, and rocking chair for one and six pence. It all only came to thirteen pounds. I came across one which was the bill for my grandmother's funeral, and that cost about twelve pounds. Three pounds for the two taxis and nine guineas for the coffin and best shroud. My mother kept all of her bills.

Mary Knox

Purse on the Railway Line

I was born in Blackburn Street. My dad came from Liverpool and my mother came from Prescot, and when I grew up I started work at the BICC. I worked there for ten years and then I got married, I had two children, a boy and a girl. I went to St Luke's Church School in Knowsley Road. We used to go Looe and Polperro for our holidays, and one year we went to the Isle of Man. We went to Rhyl one year and I lost my purse. The railway was nearby and we hunted in the caravan where we were staying, so my husband said that he would look for it the next morning. He found it in between the railway lines! There'd been trains running over it all night, but everything was intact. Another year we went fishing at Windermere – we had some fun there. But then my husband died, he was beaten up in St Helens. There were about three men who had whippets. They never caught them. It's just one of those things.

Agnes Stirrup

122

A farmhouse near Lea Green.

Married on Boxing Day

When I got married, it wasn't like getting married today. I can't believe the money that people spend to make a big show. When I got married I was twenty, and I got married on Boxing Day fifty years ago. You don't hear of people getting married on Boxing Day now. At the time I was working at Feeney's. We had the reception at home, and all the men went to the football with it

being Boxing Day, and then we had a tea at home. Where I worked at Feeney's, they supplied all of the catering for the running buffet after.

When I had children, I had one boy and two girls. The boy went to Grange Park School, the eldest girl went to a convent school, and my youngest daughter went to De la Salle School at Grange Park.

Iris Briscoe

Wembley on the Wireless

I remember the first wireless set. It sounds ridiculous now, but it was just a little box with a battery. There was a fellow named Mr Woods, and, although he was a miner, he was brilliant at making things. We were all youngsters at school, and we asked him could we listen to his wireless as 'Saints' were playing Widnes at Wembley. It was 1930. There was a brick wall at the bottom of the yard, and the wireless was placed on top of the wall. All of the kids sat round and listened, thinking what a wonderful think it was being able to listen to a game of rugby being played down at Wembley. We couldn't believe it – I wish now that I hadn't have believed it, because Widnes beat us 10-2. There's all kinds of stories still told as to why we lost that day. Some people say that the team had been out on the town the night before the match, but I don't know whether that's true or not.

Tommy Dingsdale

Liverpool Evacuees

During the Second World War we had some evacuees living with us. We were living in Rainhill, and they were from Liverpool. We had three of them living

Dr Campbell opening the British Legion Club at Sutton Oak.

The way funerals used to be in St Helens.

with us. The war was horrible. We used to go into what we called the shelter, but it was the kitchen really, and people came in to stay with us. They'd stay until the bombing was over and then they went back to their own places. The planes came over more or less ever night.

Mary Green

'Flecks'

They used to have a fellow coming around and squirting stuff so that we wouldn't get 'flecks' [fleas]. He used to come around with a cap on, and he'd give you a crack if you didn't behave – they daren't do that now.

Brenda Barrow

The 'Out Door' Was Over the Road

I used to take peelings to a lady who lived opposite my grandmas, she used to have pigs. She had a little shop, and she used to keep pigs in the back. We used to take potato peelings over to her, and she used to give us a few sweets. It was wonderful – her name, as far as I can remember, was Peg Coppel. Over the road there was the 'out door' as they called it then. I used to go with my grandma with a jug to get grandad's pint for the night.

Bessie Roughley

People Got Involved

I used to go to St Austin's School when I was young. There was a lot going on round

The way family photographs used to be taken!

Sunday School field day at Parr, St Peter's, 1959.

Thatto Heath way during the war. People used to get involved, but it didn't come that near to Thatto Heath, it was all round Liverpool and over that way. I enjoyed it, because you had a feeling in them days that there was no antagonism between people like there is now – nobody was trying to be better than anybody else. People didn't backbite with one another like they do now.

Derek Gittins

Dandelions Cured Me

I always had trouble with my chest when I was younger. I used to suffer from bronchitis and asthma, but I no longer suffer from either of those complaints. There's only one thing that cured me, and that was dandelion roots. There's milk in the dandelion roots, and we used to chew them. We'd swallow so much and then throw the rest away. I found the cure in a medical book and it worked!

John Lee

People Helped Each Other

When there were raids on, my dad always used to make us come downstairs, and I used to sleep through it. My brother and myself used to go in the bathroom, before we had

Standish Street Bridge at Pocket Nook.

the shelter. But we never went in the shelter anyway – if your name was on anything, then you would get it anyway! My dad used to come downstairs, and then there'd be a fight for who could be in the bath and make a bed there! Sometimes I just used to sleep in the armchair downstairs, and after the all clear had gone I'd go back to bed again, and next morning, I wouldn't know that I'd been up! Everybody was in the same boat, so everybody helped everyone else. It's not like it is today – they'd cut your throat for nothing. Even though there was a war on we had friends, there was always somebody there for you.

Beat Dingsdale

The Prescot Road Shoemaker

There was a young man from Ancoats, Manchester, a Jewish young man, and he was a maker of shoes – all the family made shoes. They didn't just repair shoes, they made shoes. At that time he was a young man, and in St Helens there was another chap called Marsden, and he had a daughter. They were a decent family and one of them became a doctor – we had a Doctor Marsden in St Helens. This young man came to St Helens, got to know the Marsden's, and he fell in love with their daughter, so they got married, and they had a shop just up Prescot Road on the corner – all of those shops are empty now. They lived above the shop, and they had about four or five children. They had their own governess and they were doing very well. All of the Pilkington's and all of the Greenall's, and anybody who was anybody dealt with them. In those days we had no racecourses, but they used to race horses on what they called Newton

Common, but I call it Earlestown – just where the canal is now. Anyway, he got a little bit involved with them. They kept inviting him and one thing and another, but, although he was quite well off, he wasn't in the same class as the Pilkington's. He went bankrupt, because he kept gambling. They had to come out of the shop, and they came to Haydock, and they had a little terraced house on the corner – the houses have been pulled down now. He ended up repairing shoes there, and he just couldn't stick it, so he cut his throat – he committed suicide!

Joan Gleave